BONEHILL

EVOLUTION OF A DARTMOOR HAMLET

within

Widecombe-in-the-Moor

E.H.T. WHITTEN

ryelands

First published in Great Britain in 2009

British Library Cataloguing-in-Publication Data
A CIP record for this title is available from the British Library

ISBN 978 1 906551 15 5

RYELANDS
An imprint of Halsgrove
Halsgrove House,
Ryelands Industrial Estate,
Bagley Road, Wellington, Somerset TA21 9PZ
Tel: 01823 653777   Fax: 01823 216796
email: sales@halsgrove.com

Part of the Halsgrove group of companies
Information on all Halsgrove titles is available at: www.halsgrove.com

Printed and bound by Grafiche Flaminia, Italy

Contents

DEDICATION

To all those, both the known and the many unknown,
who have been part of the evolution of Bonehill hamlet
and of this book,
and to my best friend
who made this tapestry for me.

Canvas-work copy of a roof boss, St Pancras Church,
Widecombe-in-the-Moor. Three hares or rabbits, sometimes
called the 'tinners' rabbits'. (C.S.W., 1998).

ACKNOWLEDGEMENTS

Motivation for writing this book stemmed from the pleasure of being in and around Widecombe-in-the-Moor over the past thirty years; much of the content has been accumulated slowly over this lengthy period. The largest single source of data was undoubtedly the Devon Records Office in Exeter and throughout the text reference is made to DRO followed by the specific document number; the assistance of John Draisey and his staff at DRO is gratefully acknowledged. Thanks are also due to Jenny Sanders for permission to use material from her book *Early Dartmoor Farmhouses*.

Cleo Whitten kindly helped the whole project forward by reading early drafts of the entire manuscript and especially by aiding with computer manipulation of several diagrams and photographs.

Financial support from the Dartmoor National Park Authority towards the cost of publication of this book is gratefully acknowledged.

Tim Whitten, May 2009

Middle Bonehill Farmhouse in 2009.

Widecombe's St. Pancras Church 1 km away to the west, as seen from Bonehill Lane.

INTRODUCTION

Hidden in the heart of Dartmoor, Widecombe-in-the-Moor is sometimes said to be the most visited village in England; this is undoubtedly an exaggeration, although its name is well-known throughout Britain and beyond (see *www.widecombe-in-the-moor.com*). There is a huge flux of visitors all year, as cars and coaches on the roads and in the car parks testify, despite the many narrow, tortuous, and steep access lanes. Walkers abound along the lanes and in the pubs. On the second Tuesday of each September, the traditional Fair (first recorded in October, 1850) and Uncle Tom Cobley and his grey mare attract thousands of visitors. Most visitors see and learn about only a tiny fraction of the total community and its ancient history.

As Mrs. I. M. Woods (1971, p. 254) wrote, in describing Widecombe-in-the-Moor as a parochial jigsaw, the

> village is only a tiny corner of Widecombe Parish, which is the second largest in Devon, covering near 11,000 acres [4,455 hectares] . . Widecombe is not a village at all, but a nucleus without a village. . . Holdings and farms over the whole parish are on hillsides, well chosen for sunshine and water. The holdings were all established by the middle of the sixteenth century, and by that time the really good land had been taken up, and what was left was not sufficient to make a viable holding.

Everything in, on, and about Dartmoor is inevitably evolving and has been doing so at varying rates since time out of mind. This is true of every aspect of the Moor from its geology and landforms, its weather, flora and fauna, and its human activity, to even the writing and music about Dartmoor and its variety. There have been innumerable books and articles about various aspects of Dartmoor and, possibly, even more fictional works based on a Dartmoor backdrop. Many, but not all, of these works reflect the perspective of outside observers; a few have been very specific and/or dealt with very localised areas, but most have been based on large areas of the Moor. Milton's (2006) recent *The Discovery of Dartmoor* is a good example; she embraced the whole Moor, focusing on the evolution of thinking about Dartmoor over the centuries as expressed by writers and artists who were mainly visitors or temporary residents.

The present book is wholly different. It attempts to capture a picture of the evolution of one small hamlet, Bonehill, within the encircling Moor. The hamlet lies 0.6 miles (1 km) northeast of Widecombe church, some 120 feet (36.5 m) up the eastern flank of the south-flowing East Webburn River; the East Webburn, after joining the West Webburn River, is tributary to the

Figure 1. Signatures on the 1703 Manor of Widecombe Court Roll (DRO 48/14/1/15). The nine names are printed below; *m* indicating a mark had been used, the clerk having written the actual name astride the mark. Reproduced with permission of Devon Record Office.

m John Smerdon	Elizabeth Andrew	*m* Isiar Abraham
Hugh Hamlyn	*m* William Kingwell	*m* William Caunter
m John Elliot	Gregory Windeatt	*m* Thomas Manning

River Dart. The 900-foot (274 m) contour passes through the middle of the hamlet. At this height above sea level, temperatures are commonly three or so degrees Celsius lower than in the low country of the South Hams to the south. The hamlet lies at latitude 50°34' N, and its longitude is 3°48' W.

As with a palaeontological study, the whole book has required cobbling together shreds of evidence hidden away, but awaiting discovery. In a complete investigation of the evolution of a fossilised animal community, understanding the physical nature of the animals and their local interactions is insufficient without considering the impact of changing palaeo-geography, palaeo-climate, etc. As in palaeontology, gaps inevitably remain in the evolutionary picture of Bonehill hamlet, and new vital data are unearthed unexpectedly all the time. There won't be a time when every useful fact that is potentially available has been discovered.

The history and development of Bonehill prove to be surprisingly complex. This is despite the amount still unknown - lost with the passage of time - not least because so much in earlier ages was not committed to paper, when oral traditions were all important, and many, if not all, of the populace were not literate. With a hamlet like Bonehill, physical and cultural evolution were impacted considerably by the lords of the manor (albeit usually absentee in the case of Bonehill) and changes within the county and country. Many of the complex, convoluted, and commonly extraordinarily verbose, legal documents cited in this book were signed by a mark or by a shaky scratchy hand (Fig. 1) clearly, agreements committed to by folk who were unable to read the writing for themselves.

At the outset, there are two apologies. *Firstly*, arguments could be advanced for delaying presentation of the information gathered until it is more complete. Almost every week, as this compilation progressed, new facts were stumbled upon and, not uncommonly, they modified the extant picture to some extent. For example, a mixed assortment of documents, bought at a small Tavistock auction a decade ago, contained a deed packed with precise information about Middle Bonehill Farm ownership; this deed permitted correcting some reports in the literature and illuminated an important epoch in Bonehill history. While evolutionary changes were real, but slow, throughout most of the millennium reviewed, dramatic and irreversible transformations over the past few decades have eclipsed so much. So, it seems important to present the results collated to date, before they are lost by the advancing years, especially of the author.

Secondly, the preserved data can only give a very biased picture of what Bonehill hamlet, as a living community, was really like at any particular date – we have just the skeleton without the flesh and blood. Preserved data do not capture what living in the hamlet was really like – the daily round of the indentured orphaned children, the yeoman or his wife, the servants of the lord of the manor, the blacksmith, or the scribes who wrote out all the tedious legal documents. As in palaeontology, there are more lives, events, and works irrevocably lost for ever, than were actually recorded - only some of those that are actually preserved have been unearthed to date. It would be wonderful to know what the Bonehill community was really like, but each of us can only construct a partial mental picture from the fragments that happen to be preserved and that happen to have been found. It is unrealistic to attempt painting a truly comprehensive picture or history of Bonehill hamlet, or of the Widecombe-in-the-Moor village in which it lies. So, unhappily, this book might seem disrespectful of all those lives lived which produced the hamlet that is here today.

So, this book is an attempt to marshal the available information about the background and development of the ancient and small, but vibrant, hamlet of Bonehill within its manor and village over nine, almost ten, centuries from the late tenth to the beginning of the twenty-first century CE. Some of the data has never been published before. Over such a vast period, major changes are to be expected but, in some aspects, it is surprising how much has changed but little. Most traditional life and farming on the Moor no longer exists, and the remaining buildings have changed radically over the years. Remains, records, and memories of earlier times are fast disappearing; what survives is often very dispersed and, in many cases, mere palimpsests. To aid future studies, a deliberate attempt has been made to reference fully the sources of information presented here.

It might be assumed that development of Bonehill's three old farmsteads would have been analogous; whilst there are many similarities, such an assumption would be wrong. For many decades, Middle Bonehill was owned, occupied, and farmed by successive generations of the yeoman John Smerdon family. By contrast, the contiguous and larger Lower Bonehill farmstead was, until recently, occupied and farmed by tenants (sometimes also yeomen) and

Figure 2. View from Thornhill Lane looking west over Bonehill hamlet (foreground) across the East Webburn River valley and Widecombe Church to the southern end of Hamel Down, as an imminent snow shower sweeps in from the west, 19 January 2009. In the foreground (from left to right) are the thatched Higher Bonehill, Middle Bonehill (with some of Lower Bonehill's barns beyond with red and black roofs), Bonehill House behind the tree branches, and Bonehill Cottage on the far right.

comprised a small part of huge estates owned by a succession of absentee lords. Ownership of what is now known as Lower Bonehill was the subject of bizarre inheritance and legal battles. Until the last 200 years or so, it comprised two wholly separate tenements owned by the same lord. However, the present Lower and Middle Bonehill farmhouses, both traditional Dartmoor granite long-houses, have many similarities and both were built in the late mid-sixteenth century, although the former is apparently the older. The adjacent Higher Bonehill, another very old granite farmhouse, but not a traditional long house, is younger than the other two (see Fig. 2). While an integral part of Bonehill hamlet and Widecombe Town Manor, Higher Bonehill seems to have been owned and farmed quite independently and differently from its neighbours although, of course, the crops, stock, and use of the manorial commons were much the same in each case.

Strangely, in most written accounts, Bonehill seems to have been a largely forgotten, or ignored, corner at the eastern edge of the very extensive Parish of Widecombe-in-the-Moor, despite its being only a kilometre northeast of the present village centre with its huge church and (until 2008) flourishing general store and post office. Even in the later nineteenth century, six hamlets within the Parish were commonly cited (Dunstone, Jordan, Lower Town, Ponsworthy, Poundsgate, and Venton), but not Bonehill (*cf.,* The *National Gazetteer* of 1868 and *Morris' Commercial Directory* of 1870). The scattered references that do exist tend to refer only to Bonneyhill, Bonhill, Bunhill, or Bunhill Farm, etc., (or occasionally Bonehill), without differentiating between the four discrete farmsteads (later only three), so detective work is needed to piece the history together.

While some of Bonehill's homesteads and field boundaries have withstood the onslaught of time, the way they are used has changed for ever. Perhaps, more importantly, the way of thinking, and the horizons and expectations, of successive (and recently declining) generations have changed so dramatically that it is difficult to picture the social life and organisation of the past decades (let alone the past centuries). Inevitably, current thinking about past generations tends to be distorted by 'twenty-first-century spectacles' (eye-glasses), because everyone today has been moulded by familiarity with the internal combustion engine, health-and-safety regulations, sexual expectations, electricity and television, global competition, changed religious and social values, etc.

Those lucky enough to have survived eight or so decades remember building wheat or hay ricks; the harvest tossed up by pitchfork, having been gathered by horse-drawn wains from adjacent small fields. Eight or ten laboured on these tasks in an attempt to beat the ever-changeable weather. Today, with the advent of tractors and big machinery, things are different. Although Dartmoor terrain, soil, and climate do not invite modern satellite-controlled combine harvesters, field sizes have steadily increased, and arable and cereal crops have largely disappeared; the labour force maintaining the households, sustained by farming, and providing ancillary services has been decimated.

Today, we all know where Dartmoor is and regularly consult satellite-corrected computer-generated maps before driving (*via* patchily council-maintained asphalt roads) to another village 150 miles (240 km) away. What was it like to live on Dartmoor in the mid-19th century when roads and even wheeled horse-drawn vehicles were unknown in some parts? The first printed Ordnance Survey map of the Widecombe area was issued in 1809, shortly after the Napoleonic War. Matthew Paris' map of Great Britain (Fig. 6) shows what visual guidance the sparse long-distance travellers received in 1250; in those days, visual portrayal of the land about one was essentially non-existent. The famous circular world map (52 inches, 1.32 m, in diameter) preserved on a wall of Hereford Cathedral – with Jerusalem at the centre and Britain nestling

Figure 3. Small part of map of the British Isles, *Tabula Nova Hibernie Anglie Et Scotie*, compiled by the German cartographer Waldseemüller in 1505-7 and printed (from a wood block) in a new atlas in Strassburg in 1513; the ports of Bristol (Eristo), Dartmouth (Artamua), and Plymouth (Premua) are shown clearly. From a private collection; reproduced with permission.

near the circumference – illustrated for all to see what the world was supposed to be like on the basis of the current religious (Christian) belief. Kline's (2001) fully illustrated book, although somewhat controversial, gives a good impression of that venerated map and educated peoples' thinking in the thirteenth century.

The English transcription of beautifully-illustrated manuscripts written about 1220-1250 and published as *Bestiary, or the Book of Beasts* (Barber, 1992), gives a vivid insight into the medieval mind and thinking about the fantastic supposed animals of the natural world and their religious significance. Sir John Mandeville's account of his 34-year travels (*e.g.*, Coleman, 2006) through the Middle East, the East Indies, China, and Mongolia beginning in 1322 seems wholly unreal when read today, but it is the source of many fanciful images (*e.g.*, headless human islanders) that embellished the borders of seventeenth century printed maps and informed the contemporary world. Mandeville's whole account reflected a world bounded by fantasy, superstition, and dread, at a time when most Englishmen probably regarded a visit to the next village or town as a major event. The so-called Gough map in the Bodleian Library, Oxford, is an amazingly realistic portrayal of Great Britain drawn on two pieces of animal hide at approximately 1:1,000,000 scale. It was drawn around about 1360 for some royal purpose but it is not known by whom or where, and it is probably an updated version of a map produced late in the previous century; accurate distances – distances as the crow flies – between many named towns are shown (Millea, 2007, p. 32). Of course, until recently extremely few eyes would ever have fallen on this masterpiece – indeed, very few people in the fourteenth and fifteenth centuries could have comprehended what the drawing represents. Many years passed before a more-realistic 'modern' *printed* map of the British Isles appeared, the first being compiled by the German cartographer Waldseemüller between 1505-7 on the basis of rather older Italian sea charts; the English south coast, more frequented by mariners, was the most realistic part (Fig. 3) and showed the ports of Dartmouth (Artamua), Plymouth (Premua), and Bristol (Eristo). Sebastian Münster, often called one of the most influential cartographers of the sixteenth century, produced in 1540 a beautiful woodcut map of North and South America printed in Switzerland, but its sole illustration of human activity is not exactly inviting (Fig. 4).

Figure 4. The sole sign of humanity in North and South America shown by Münster 1540. Small part of the map *Die neüwe Inselen* from the 1544 German edition of the atlas. From a private collection; reproduced with permission.

The material presented in the following pages is divided into four main sections.

1. Features of the rural scene generally at the time of the Normal Conquest (1086) – a background which probably remained relatively little changed for centuries; apart from the Domesday Book records, very little evidence remains about Widecombe-in-the-Moor at that time.

2. Changes within the next six hundred years – although places like Plymouth, Exeter, and Dartmouth developed as major trade centres and particularly the prosperous city of Exeter (Kowaleski, 1995), communication with the isolated uplands of Dartmoor was only on foot or horse-back, so change there was modest, although tin mining and wool production brought substantial prosperity to the Widecombe-area community for many years and fostered considerable interaction with the stannery and mills of Ashburton. The rebuilding of Widecombe's fine St. Pancras church reflects considerable expense. Remains of compact stone houses and other buildings of a medieval hamlet at some 400 meters (almost 1,100 feet) above sea-level south-east of Hound Tor reflect a viable farming community that was abandoned in the mid-14th century. Probably similar hamlets flourished in the more protected valleys around Widecombe but, to date, remnants have not been located except for the obvious medieval field boundaries described in Chapter 2 (*cf.*, Butler, 1991, pp. 54-56). The extensive building of granite long-houses and associated granite out-buildings throughout the Parish of Widecombe-in-the-Moor reflects increased affluence amongst the lords of the manors and those farming in the area.

3. The complex sequence of changes in lordship of the Manor of Widecombe in the years around 1700 - these profoundly influenced evolution of tenements within the Parish, although contemporary people living in them may have been largely unaware of most of these events. The transition from the Pole family to the Cabells, and then *via* the D'Oylys to the Wottons occurred over only a few years. Within an even shorter period, a sequence of Wottons became Lord of the Manor before most of their Widecombe estates became held by three trustees for 99 years to provide funds for an infant child who had become the sole heir of Rev. John Wotton in 1746; complications stemming from the trust established on John Wotton's death materially affected the future of Widecombe-in-the-Moor.

4. Development of life and farming in Bonehill hamlet between the mid-seveteenth century and 2000, as traced through scattered documentary evidence that enables the ownership, occupiers, and utilisation of the farmsteads to be traced. Despite considerable changes of owners and tenants of the other estates and tenements, and the widespread mobility of a large part of the population, Middle Bunhill Farm was owned and occupied by successive John Smerdons for decades until 1869, when it was sold at auction.

This, of course, is only the recent history involving less than a quarter of the period represented by visible evidence of human occupation and agricultural activity on Dartmoor. The area around Widecombe has a rich history of farming stretching back to the centuries immediately before the second millennium BCE., when the settled population apparently began to increase. Even today, several thousand hut circles survive across Dartmoor and evidence a significant population which lived in a more wooded landscape than characterises Dartmoor today. Later, the population declined towards the end of the second millennium BCE., probably because of a less hospitable climate. Archaeological evidence about the houses and fields of these prehistoric farmers abounds across the higher ground of Dartmoor, as illustrated graphically by Butler's (1991) detailed maps and aerial photographs.

Anglo-Saxon Wessex was apparently divided into *shires* (units of national administration) before the end of the eighth century, each shire being divided into *hundreds*, administrative units with courts for taxation purposes, maintenance of peace and order, and the settlement of local pleas (*cf.*, Stenton, 1971, pp. 292-9). So, even remote areas around Widecombe lay within a clearly defined hundred; they were also within the vast Peadington estate, defined by the Peadington Charter. Herdsmen from lowland farmsteads to the south of Dartmoor undoubtedly drove stock up the Dart and Webburn river valleys for summer grazing on the moorland. In late Saxon times, individual farmers also appear to have begun returning to settle and farm land up to 900 feet or so above sea level. Although some of the stone walls and ditches of the old Bronze Age rectangular field boundaries were reused and can still be identified, most pre-medieval evidence in the valley bottoms and sides has been overprinted by more recent farming development. After some 400 years of Saxon colonisation, clearing, and open-field farming, the population of Devon was some 70,000, according to estimates based on 1086 data in the Domesday Book, making it the thirteenth English county in terms of population density. Although there is little direct evidence, Hoskins (1954, pp. 49, 57-8) suggested that, high on the edges of the moorland, some hamlets and farmsteads had probably been in continuous use since Romano-British times, or even earlier. The hundreds were still shown on numerous seventeenth century printed maps.

Note about spelling the names of places and people.

The correct spelling of place names in and around Widecombe-in-the-Moor is difficult. While Widecombe-in-the-Moor is the official name today, and there is another Widecombe in Devon, most residents commonly say they live in Widecombe; there have been many spellings in the past (*e.g.*, Withicombe, Wythekon). For histories of various parts of the world, authors have often decided to use only present-day spelling. However, part of the mystique of Widecombe and Bonehill is the dialect and the spelling.

Almost every nearby village, hamlet and tenement has been (and still is) variously spelled over the past five centuries; not infrequently, the same place is differently spelled in the numerous legal documents – even in the same document. Again, successive legal indentures merely used Bonneyhill to refer to a lease or a sale of wholly different tenements within what is today Bonehill hamlet. Bonehill is only a recent version of the ancient hamlet's name. Spitchwick is a manor diversely spelled in old documents (*e.g.*, Spechewyke) and what is now Blackaton Manor is referred to as Blagdon-Pipard (very variously spelled) in most documents more than a couple of decades old. Similar remarks apply to people's names. One of the more obvious problems concerns members of the D'Oyly family, whose name is not infrequently spelled differently within a single legal document. Is their name really Doyly, Doyley, D'oyly, or D'Oyly? Complications of this sort are not limited to the past; today, Widecombe is often miswritten Widdecombe or Widdicombe, while a man born and living in Devon, a Devonian, is an Englishman living in Great Britain, who will probably say he's British and know he is a citizen of the United Kingdom.

In the following chapters, many of the varied spellings are preserved, while trying to ensure there is no confusion about the actual place or family involved. This emphasises both the evolution and the difficulties of unravelling which properties and people were alluded to in individual documents. Historical understanding is not helped by successive generations, at all levels of society, frequently having identical given names. Also, within Widecombe-in-the-Moor there were (and still are) numerous families with the same family name (surname). This is all part of Bonehill and Widecombe!

1
AFTER THE NORMAN CONQUEST

No archaeological evidence has been found of Roman activity on Dartmoor. Isca Dumnoniorum (present–day Exeter) was served from the east by the Fosse Way and there is evidence that the Romans penetrated around the north of Dartmoor and thence to Cornwall. They built a road southward from Exeter that reached towards Teignbridge and possibly Mount Batten, Plymouth. Amery (1925, p. 46) noted there have been "rather frequent discoveries of coins of Claudius, Decius and other emperors" in Ashburton. Todd (2000, p. 81, map 11.1) showed the known courses of Roman road fragments north-east and east of Dartmoor, while Maxfield's (2000, p. 78, map 10.1) map included known Roman forts between Okehampton and Exeter. Moreland and Bannister (1993, p. 25) suggested that, in general, by the Middle Ages the decayed Roman roads in England were amongst the worst in Europe.

Quite well-reasoned arguments suggest that the Peadington landscore (dating from the 8th to 10th century) enumerated the bounds of a large Saxon estate which embraced most of present-day Widecombe-in-the-Moor and much of Ashburton, Ilsington, and Manaton (see Davidson, 1876; Cocks, 1970, p.77; Brewer, 2002, pp. 299, *et seq.*); Brewer (2002, p. 301) provided a sketch map of the supposed boundary of the Peadington estate (Fig. 5); Pike (1993, pp. 53-5) earlier showed maps of possible different northern boundaries for the Paedington (*sic*) estate in early and in later Saxon times. Future research may produce further details of these Saxon estates but, currently, it is not easy to visualise what physical living conditions and communications were like in the middle of Dartmoor in either Saxon times or during the Norman Conquest. However, the first glimmers of documented history for the civil parish of Widecombe-in-the-Moor, and the hamlet of Bonehill (which lies near its eastern margin) date back to the reign of King Edward the Confessor (1042-1066).

It must be emphasised that this chapter is almost wholly based on secondary sources – published works of scholars who, in the main, were primarily interested in other areas of England. Surprisingly little of specifically Widecombe early history has been collated in an accessible form; because of its isolation and topography, it is likely that its evolution and characteristics differed from those of the rest of England, and even the rest of Devon. A study of the manor of Jordan (Lineham, 1962) showed what can sometimes be uncovered by hunting for and interpreting ancient documentary sources. It is hoped that material assembled here may stimulate further search for specific local data about the evolution of this unique part of Dartmoor.

The following account owes much to Maitland's (1897) *Domesday Book and Beyond*. Maitland was Downing Professor of the Laws of England in the University of Cambridge. Lord Acton, Regius Professor of History at Cambridge, described him as the ablest historian of his time in England (cover of Maitland's 1897 book, 1960 edition). Although some of Maitland's conclusions about 11th century England have been modified or

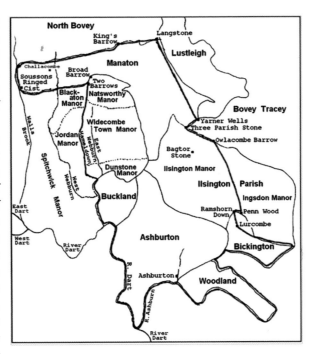

Figure 5. Possible boundary (blue line) of the Peadington Estate in the 8th to 10th centuries, defined in relation to more recent manors and parishes (adapted from Brewer, 2002, p. 301, Fig. 102).

questioned by more-recent scholars, and some conclusions are still debatable, most represent accepted learning (Miller, 1960).

A statement like the "... holdings were all established by the middle of the 16th century ..." (quoted from Woods, 1971, in the Introduction) is deceptive and could give a false sense of understanding of what it was like at that time; similarly, with the manors recorded in the Domesday records of 1086. In fact, it is difficult to imagine life in the medieval environment, although, of course, gross aspects of topography -- the tors and valleys -- are largely unchanged; the frontiers of cultivation, especially of the higher ground, have waxed and waned several times over the centuries. Most inhabitants of the Widecombe area in the 11th century were undoubtedly peasant farmers, dependent almost wholly for daily needs on their own fields and livestock, managed with very primitive technology. Dependence on the weather and vulnerability to disease must have resulted in prolonged shortages and widespread malnutrition. With extremely limited communication and transportation, and primitive husbandry, the extended family, slaves, and livestock on each holding had to produce enough food for the whole year. To be viable, enough land was needed to cater for years of poor, as well as good, harvests. The virtual lack of medical knowledge meant that minor infections, diseases, and accidental injuries (fractures, etc.) would have frequently led to permanent disability or premature death. In addition to natural unavoidable mishaps, human violence was probably common, with quarrels and disputes readily leading to the use of knives or other weapons. It was a restless time in England; in the three centuries after 1066, there was only one period lasting more than 30 years that was free of civil wars or civil disturbances, although such upheavals may have rarely caused ripples up on the Moor around Widecombe. Illiteracy was the norm in England, with less than one in ten people across the country being able to read or write, and still fewer doing so with facility. Life expectancy must have been very short. Even by 1300, life expectancy of nobles' children in England at birth was only 22 - 28 years; a poor man in his 20s could expect to live into his forties (*cf.*, Miller & Hatcher 1978, p. vii, *et seq.*)

Kingship, land tax (geld), and shire courts were all products of Anglo-Saxon heritage in England. Since 975, or earlier, formal land registers seem to have existed which recorded:

> (i) land tax due from each administrative hundred within each county,
> (ii) individual tenure of land by lordship within each county, and
> (iii) land-tax liability of each lordship.

Such sophistication implies use of standardised assessment units for land (hides). Then, at the beginning of one of the most dynamic periods in recorded Western European history, came the conquest of the Christian Kingdom of England by aliens, speaking a foreign language but also Christian, who imposed a new land-tenure and financial system on the land (Loyn, 1987, p. 3, *et seq.*).

Thus, in 1066, the Normans inherited literate, active, and continuous administrations at county level that maintained lists of tenants-in-chief and efficiently assessed and collected land taxes. Throughout England, a structured and tiered feudal society of lords and men was well entrenched; the men in each tier owed homage to a superior in the next higher tier, with the king at the apex of the pyramid. The structure was very flat by present-day standards. The farmers, labourers, and slaves seldom had more than two lords between them and King Edward, but the structure became steadily more complex under the Normans; under King William there might well have been three lords in the chain. In each of the two or three hierarchical tiers, personal dependence was enshrined in homage. This was exemplified by a knight becoming a baron's 'man' through an oath of homage, or 'men' owing services and various obligations, due to their personal dependence on their lord, stemming from the giving and receiving of land which created dependent tenants of the lord. In medieval society, such hierarchy and degree were held to have divine approval, which distinguished between individuals according to their role and function. Indeed, shortly before the Norman Conquest, it had been written that the king's throne was supported by those who toiled (providing sustenance, ploughmen, husbandmen), those who prayed (spiritual toil for the benefit of all), and those who fought (guarding towns and country against enemies).

After becoming king, William distributed the relatively small discrete estates which already existed to his followers; the new overlords commonly held several manors scattered over a considerable area. In what is now Widecombe-in-the-Moor Parish, for example, according to the Domesday records, Depdona (Jordan) Manor was held by William de Falaise with the larger Chochintona Manor (Cockington, near Torquay).

What we now know as land 'freehold' did not then exist, because all land was held of someone else who demanded rent and/or service for it (Miller & Hatcher, 1978, p. xi). Hence, both personal and land-tenure dependence bound society together by entailed binding obligations upon everyone (*e.g.*, war service to the king by barons; compulsory farm labour for the lord by unfree peasants who were attached for life to their holding; rent payments in money and kind; seeking permission and paying fines for educating or marrying off children).

The Survey that led to the Domesday Book

Everyone has heard of the Domesday Book. Although difficult to interpret, it is a vast store of accurate and precise knowledge about 11th century England. It comprised two volumes in Latin; the first dealt with all English counties except Essex, Norfolk, and Suffolk, which were addressed in the second volume (the Little Domesday). In addition, the Exeter Domesday (*Liber* Exoniensis or Exon.) is preserved in Exeter Cathedral; it includes slightly different information for the south-western counties and includes estates' livestock data omitted from the main, or Exchequer, Domesday Book (Exch.). The full Exch. and Exon. texts for Devon have been translated into English (*e.g*, Devon. Assoc., 1884-1892; Thorn and Thorn, 1985); the several holdings within what is now the Parish of Widecombe-in-the-Moor are detailed below.

These Domesday texts have provoked much debate. Maitland (1897, pp. 23, 48) argued that the Domesday survey was conducted so that taxation could be just and under a uniform system, and also to determine whether more land tax (geld) could be raised than previously. However, more-recent scholarship suggests that, if Domesday Book is in some sense a tax register, it is much more obviously a land register recording ownership (Davis, 1987, p. 15). From the 1st to the 11th centuries CE, assessments or surveys (known as *descriptiones*, from the Latin *descriptio*) were made of many parts of Europe. However, the Domesday survey is unique amongst European '*descriptiones*' in citing property values – actually, values in King Edward's time, later, and again when the survey was made in 1086. For each county, compilers arranged the data carefully under the correct tenant-in-chief. The compilation was possible, not because of extraordinary Norman genius, but because of the extraordinary nature of the Conquest. Having conquered the whole country, all land was at King William's disposal and he gave estates with their inhabitants to whomever he pleased, thereby rewarding his followers with the lands of dispossessed Anglo-Saxons (Davis, 1987, pp. 15, 21-4). For Domesday, the Normans tried to convert the diverse regional English society and units of measurement to a common terminology familiar to them; although unable to eliminate all variations across the country, the Survey indicates clearly the work of a single controlling mind (Holt, 1987).

Holt (1987) argued persuasively in favour of Wright's (1730) perspective of the Domesday survey, rather than Maitland's (1897) interpretation of it being a geld (land-tax) book. Because so much land had been redistributed by the King, there was a pressing need to record the tenements and for the new tenants to perform homage, thereby affirming their obligations. It is clear that homage was considered a reciprocal act, done in return for something real, actual or expected, with homage and tenure normally going together (Holt, 1987, p. 58). In consequence, the actual survey was announced at Gloucester by the King at Christmas 1085, with the intention of it being completed in time for the main land-holding men to perform homage for their recorded tenements on 1st August, 1086 (Holt, 1987, p. 56). In an accurate and carefully cross-referenced compilation, the Domesday survey provided a quick reference to the location and tenure of every manor; at a deeper level, it addressed resources, values, potential, and land-tax assessment (Holt, 1987, p. 55). By homage on 1st August, 1086, King William strengthened his feudal rights and tenants gained a recorded warranty of their tenure, probably, in many cases, for the first time (Holt, 1987, p. 60). The vast land book thus achieved stability by putting a final seal on the Norman occupation; some tenants gained and some no doubt lost in the exercise, but the royal record continued to be used to determine tenure for a couple of centuries (Holt, 1987, p. 56). Within a century, the survey was dubbed *The Domesday Book.*

Hoskins (1954, p. 55) pointed out that many Celtic place names in Devon existed for centuries before the Norman Conquest, "... but Domesday includes them silently under another heading"; it was mainly the manors that were recorded, while hamlets and farmsteads beyond the demesnes (lords' home farms) are commonly not identified.

The magnitude of the Survey cannot be over estimated. It intermingled existing written data from local courts with information obtained from land holders, all confirmed by juries of the hundreds in the county courts (Holt, 1987, p. 45). The Survey could not have been made without the barons' co-operation; they could have been obstructive, but it was to their advantage to co-operate (Davis, 1987, p. 27).

For Devon (and several other south-western counties) the separate *inquisito geldi* (prepared in about 1083-4) provided information on land taxes by hundred.

Those who worked on the land

For the area now known as the Parish of Widecombe-in-the-Moor, Domesday referred to manors having villeins, bordars, and serfs. People were either born free or unfree, and that status was quite independent of their landholding. The Domesday survey recorded some 25,000 serfs in England; they comprised a definite class, close to slaves which, in general, had virtually no legal rights. It can be assumed that a serf was often a house servant; he may have had property such as a cottage with yardland which he might have called his own; he may even have had some oxen and a plot of arable land, labouring for himself as well as on specific duties for his lord (Maitland, 1897, p. 59). There were probably few legal limitations to the masters' power and serfs were commonly annexed to (a subordinate part of) a tenement with specific required duties.

In the early 12th century, somewhat later, a clear distinction was maintained between freemen and serfs. Thus, Maitland (1897, pp. 56-7) wrote that *Leges Henrici* indicated:

> A serf becomes such either by birth or by some event, such as a sale into slavery, that happens in his lifetime. Servile blood is transmitted from father to child; some lords hold that it is also transmitted by mother to child. If a slave is to be freed this should be done publicly, in court, or church or market, and lance and helmet or other the arms of free men should be given him, while he should give his lord thirty pence, that is the price of his skin, as a sign that he is henceforth 'worthy of his hide'. On the other hand, when a free man falls into slavery then also there should be a public ceremony. He should put his head between his lord's hands and should receive as the arms of slavery some bill-hook or the like... But, to come to the fundamental rule, the villanus, the meanest of free men, is a two-hundred-man, that is to say, if he be slain the very substantial wergild of 200 Saxon shillings or £4 must be paid to his kinsfolk, while a man-bot of 30 shillings is paid to his lord. But, if a servus [serf] be slain his kinsfolk receive the comparatively trifling sum of 40 pence while the lord gets the man-bot of 20 shillings.

According to pre-Norman tradition, a villein was not tied to the soil and might acquire five hides and also thegn-right (see below). In Norman times, a villeins' land and oxen seem to have had rights protected by law. The small man-bot, just mentioned as being payable to the lord if a villein was killed, suggests that everything a villein owned did not belong to his lord (Maitland, 1897, p. 82). Villeins were quite a varied group ranging from men who, or whose ancestors, owned their land under the King's political authority, to those (or who's ancestors) had always been tenants of another's land (Maitland, 1897, p. 87). Thus, some villeins were much wealthier than others, and some were probably economically subject to other villeins (Maitland, 1897, p. 67).

The Domesday book frequently listed bordars separately from villeins. Bordars appear to have been an economically defined, inferior type of villein, although the distinction remains unclear. The term bordar is of French origin and never took firm root in England. A distinction, depending upon the amount of land possessed or the amount of service done, cannot be formulated accurately but, in the Domesday record, the average holding of a villein was about one quarter of a hide, while bordars had less (Maitland, 1897, p. 66).

Because of the personal character of serfdom, unfree men were bought and sold, and early Norman lords could use the royal courts and administration to recover their fugitive villeins; in law, a villein's goods and chattels were his lord's (Miller & Hatcher, 1978, pp. 113-5). Most commonly, villeins were probably sold or given away with the tenements they held, although documents prove that there was a market in villeins quite apart from villein tenements. As late as 1276, Glastonbury Abbey was granted a man at Shepton Mallet, Somerset, with his chattels and his progeny as a serf and a villein born. The villeins had to cultivate the manorial demesnes; the unfree tenants normally owed rent (in money and kind), seasonal work (boons) like ploughing, harvesting, and fencing, and also week work (work on the lord's land for a specified number of days per week) (Miller & Hatcher, 1978, p. 121). Unfree tenants paid fines to marry off daughters or if their daughters were detected in immorality; fees were also involved before sons could be sent to school or could enter the church (Miller & Hatcher, 1978, p. 117). By contrast, unlike a villein, a free tenant and his holdings and goods were safeguarded (Miller & Hatcher, 1978, p. 118).

Measurements and sizes of land and holdings

There is no convincing evidence for Roman roads having penetrated Dartmoor, although their roads passed north and south of the Moor (*cf.*, Groves, 1970, p. 184). The Saxons invaded Devon in the 7th century and, in the following six centuries, many farms and villages were settled and woodlands cleared. Many Devon parish boundaries were drawn in early Saxon times; for example, Lydford was founded in the 9th century and Tavistock Abbey in about 974 (Groves, 1970, pp. 183-6).

Before 1066, there could have been little precise, though much nominal, uniformity in land measurement in England (Maitland, 1897, p. 428). In Venerable Bede's day (673-735), each free family (each taxpayer) typically had no more and no less than a hide of land. 'Manor' is an inappropriate term for such tenements, although nominally they comprised 120 acres and probably each had a few slaves to help till them. Coagulations of three or four such (not necessarily adjacent) tenements might have approached manorial status under a minor nobleman; such holdings would probably have been cultivated by the estate-owners' slaves and freedmen (*cf.*, Maitland, 1897, p. 596).

By Anglo-Saxon times in the 11th century, an estate of five hides was an adequate endowment for a thegn. Thegns were generally warriors who held, sometimes jointly with others (coparceners), land required to supply a warrior for the King's service. Although all of the King's thegns had a clearly defined legal status, the richer, higher-status, thegns dealt directly with the King, paying their taxes and obligations directly to him, while poorer thegns were under the sheriff administratively (Maitland, 1897, p. 205). At a lower level, a Domesday thegn was apparently commonly someone who held land in return for the ongoing performance of specified service to his immediate lord (Campbell, 1987, p. 212).

Maitland (1897, p. 546) concluded that, to the Domesday surveyors, a hide was always 120 acres in fiscal terms, but not necessarily in terms of actual land; he claimed that, at its worst, the fiscal hide "... is jobbery; at its best a lame compromise between a unit of area and a unit of value".

Before the Normal Conquest, the human foot, the measuring stick (rod, pole, or perch), and a day's ploughing were the basic land-measurement units. The only larger unit was the hide, the arable land with appurtenances of one family or householder; because of its general similarity across England, the hide seems to have become a unit of measure.

Subdivision of arable land was dominated by the fact that, ploughing a strip of land 40 rods (one furlong) long and four rods wide with a team of eight oxen by noon, was a normal fair-day's work; such a piece of land was an acre. After noon, the oxen had to go to pasture (Maitland, 1897, p. 438). Maitland (1897, p. 449) suggested the acre would not have become a unit of measure unless the method of ploughing was fairly uniform across England. The customary length of a furrow (40 rods) in open country would have been controlled by the oxen's endurance, and this led to fields being divided into contiguous parallel acre strips one furlong long (40 perches) and nominally four perches wide. In practice, width depended upon furrow spacing; local conditions led to smaller or larger areas being ploughed by noon. Maitland (1897, p. 442) opined that to suggest that a shorter actual acre was not really an acre would have been like telling a farmer his foot was not a real foot because it is less than 12 inches (*ca.* 30.5 cm). Today, a furlong is one-eighth of a mile (*i.e.*, 201 m), and one acre is *ca.* 0.4 ha.

One rod is nominally 16.5 feet (5.03 m), but it is doubtful whether this was standardised before the 12th century (Maitland, 1897, p. 436). Adjusting to topography meant some furlongs (plough lengths) were longer than others, so acres differed in size in different areas. Throughout the Middle Ages, actual acres across England were quite variable in size; over time, it became accepted that an acre need not be ten times as long as it is broad (Maitland, 1897, p. 447). In medieval documents, ideal acres are used in addition to acres that were actually found in the field; naturally, the same applies to hides because each is 120 acres of arable land.

Being accustomed to accurate maps and plans in the 21st century, it is difficult to comprehend the difficulties of defining landed property several centuries before even primitive maps had been made. Admittedly, the Romans had produced a remarkably accurate map of the 50,000 or more miles (*ca.* 80,500 km) of road in their empire in about the 3rd century CE, but roads were only shown as straight lines with all land features distorted around them. As mentioned, by the Middle Ages, the decayed Roman roads in Britain are said to have been amongst the worst in Europe; by that time, roads were more often than not "... narrow winding lanes or bridle tracks between cultivated fields and, in the absence of hedges and fences, frequently changed courses as weather conditions or changes in land ownership dictated" (Moreland and Bannister, 1993, p. 25). In about 1250, some 35 years after the signing of *Magna Carta*, Matthew Paris, a Benedictine monk at St Albans, drew the first English map currently preserved. This picturesque map of England, Wales, and Scotland (Fig. 6), included in his *History of the English*, was not intended as a true geographical representation in the modern sense. Although it showed rivers and a few river crossings, town positions are distorted to lie in an almost straight line, to show travellers the shortest route to Dover and thus to the Continent; while Devonia and Cornubia are clearly labelled, no clear relationships with the County of Devon are indicated.

Figure 6. Matthew Paris' Map of Great Britain prepared about 1250; apparently drawn as an itinerary to show pilgrims the route to Dover and thus to the Continent. It was constructed around the towns aligned north-to-south down the centre of the map. The map is preserved in the British Museum. (Reproduced with permission of the British Library.)

Manors

Long before the Norman Conquest, the hide became a unit in the unwieldy English taxation system (Maitland, 1897, p. 419); a hide is four virgates. Although greatly corrupted in actual use, the underlying theory was that a typical Anglo-Saxon householder or taxpayer had one hide, that is something close to 120 acres, of arable land which is the amount that an eight-oxen team could plough. It is likely that, in most cases, such a householder (or manorial lord) kept about a third of his land in demesne, while the remainder was worked by subservient tenants. Although the original hide referred to the extent of arable land only, it implicitly involved ploughing by oxen and thus pasture rights too. In general, pasture land was not individually owned; beasts were turned out on the vill's commons. For everyday needs, every village must have been essentially self-sufficient, having an equilibrium between arable and pasture, although tax assessment was on the arable land alone (Maitland, 1897, p. 450).

By current standards, late Saxon and Norman England would seem undeveloped and backward, with considerable land and labour being used to maintain a very small population. However, contemporary Flemish accounts noted England's fertile fields, its herds, fish, and wildfowl; this richness sustained considerable expansion in the 10th century.

The term *manor* (*manerium*, or in Exon. Domesday Book, *mansio*) seems to have been introduced to England by the Normans (although other derivations of the Latin verb *manere* were used earlier by English scribes to represent the distinctly different concept of the English hide) (Maitland, 1897, p. 141). Maitland (1897, p. 143) contended that *manerium* (*mansio*), for which we have to use manor, was a technical term in the Norman taxation system. Palmer (1987) agreed with Maitland, but pointed out that manors are differentiated clearly from other types of holding, manors being where geld was collected, whereas vills with no manor were subordinate to a manor in a neighbouring vill.

A manor recorded in Domesday did not necessarily contain demesne lands (*i.e.*, land occupied by the owner, rather than by tenants, etc.), have a court of its own, or have freehold tenants. Rather, a manor seems to have been a parcel of land recognised for geld (land tax) and each manor's geld was assessed in terms of hides, acres, etc., which may, or may not, have matched precisely the actual geographical areas. The Domesday manor was "... a block of landed property managed as a single unit from a particular centre ... [and] the manorial framework was a landowning and land-management grid superimposed on the settlement pattern of villages and hamlets" (Miller & Hatcher, 1978, pp. 19-20). Across England, there was considerable variation in the structure of manors; some were vast, but others "... consisted solely of demesne located in a single village; in others, parcels of demesne were scattered over other villages or hamlets at some distance from the main manorial centre. ... there were demesneless manors composed only of peasant tenements" (Miller & Hatcher, 1978. p.20).

It seems that each county was assessed on a certain number of hides, which were then apportioned among the hundreds, and then again amongst its vills, and again to holdings within each vill; a round number of hides, virgates, or acres tended to be assigned at each of these stages. Hence, for fiscal purposes, each holding was a manor, or part of a manor, and it contained (or was deemed to contain) specific hides, virgates, and/or acres; the occupier may have been a serf or villein having a lord, and that lord paid homage to a more-important lord. When the sovereign awarded a manor or manors to a lord, the award was of the land including the tenants, serfs, etc. occupying it. The overlords were probably responsible for paying the land tax (geld), but exacted payments (in money or kind) from those who occupied their land. Some of the overlords' land could be privileged and exempted by the King from geld (Maitland, 1897, pp. 153-4).

Jones (1987, p. 200) asserted that, for England as a whole,

> the positive information provided by Domesday Book, when it can be tested against other near contemporary evidence, is usually correct and reliable. ... the disposition of arable land ... seems to provide a better pointer both to the broad pattern and to the scale of settlement. The record of ploughlands probably represented a new fiscal assessment ... to record the actual amount of arable land held by all sorts and conditions of men.

Although corroborative contemporary data for Dartmoor are not available, the general reliability of Domesday may be expected to apply. Across southwest England, manors with only some 60 arable acres were common. In the west-country, such small manors frequently seem to have been consolidated under a wealthy landlord, perhaps a thegn before the Conquest, or a Norman baron later, although each little holding was still reported as a manor in the Domesday survey.

Taxation

Before the Norman Conquest in 1066, geld, or land tax, was levied sporadically in England by the monarchs; the earliest surviving written record shows that £10,000 tribute was paid to the Danes in the year 991; in ensuing years, geld was levied occasionally as a war tax. King William I recognised that among "... the most valuable of his newly acquired regalia [was] a right to levy a land-tax under the name of geld or danegeld." (Maitland, 1897, p. 25). Maitland (1897, p. 26) recorded that

> No sooner was William crowned [December 1066] than 'he laid on men a geld exceeding stiff.' In the next year 'he set a mickle geld' on the people. In the winter of 1083-4 he raised a geld of 72 pence (6 Norman shillings) upon the hide. That this tax was enormously heavy is plain.

Details of the latter tax are incorporated in the Exeter *Inquisito Geldi* of 1083-4 which lists geldable land, its holders, and the geld that could be raised from it. Haytor Hundred (in which Widecombe-in-the-Moor lies) was then called Carsewilla Hundred comprising 50 hides. King William received £9 12s.0d. for 32 of these hides*. Of the 50 hides, the King

---

* s. = shilling and d. = pence; in pre-decimalised UK currency, 12d. = 1s., and 20s. = £1.

and his barons held 16 in demesne free of geld (the King one hide, a bishop and two abbots just over seven hides, and eight barons just over eight hides); by tradition, the King received no tax (geld) from two other hides, one held by the Fegadri (tax collectors) and the other by Hamelin (under the Earl Mortain). Interestingly, of the Domesday manors within what is now Widecombe-in-the-Moor Parish, one was held by the King himself and one each by four powerful barons who held demesnes in Carsewilla Hundred free of geld (Devon. Assoc., 1884-1892, p. *xl*). Owing to privileges and immunities granted capriciously over the decades, and to a radically vicarious method of determining geldable acres of the counties and hundreds, assessments appear to have been full of anomalies and inequities (Maitland, 1893, p. 26).

According to Maitland (1893, Table I, pp. 64-5), Domesday book tended to record for each manor:

A. The geld (or land tax) rating in terms of (in Devon) hides, virgates, and/or acres of arable land (a total of 1,119 hides being recorded for Devon).

B. The amount of arable land for the recorded number of plough teams or plough oxen, always assuming eight oxen to a team (in Devon, *ca.* 7,972 teamlands were recorded, *i.e.*, a total of 7,962 ploughs were needed to work the land).

C. The number of plough teams belonging to the lord and/or other occupants of the manor (*ca.* 5,542 teams across the whole of Devon).

In analysing data for the whole of England, Maitland (1897, p. 533) concluded the fiscal value of an average teamland across the southernmost counties of England in 1086 decreased steadily from east to west, so that in Cornwall the value was only one-sixth that in Kent. In consequence, with any justice, Devon could not be taxed at the same rate per acre as, say, Wiltshire. Maitland concluded that every test of Domesday data indicated the extreme poverty of Devon and Cornwall at that time, and he believed that relative poverty continued throughout the Middle Ages.

Using averages, the values of **B** and **C** (above) are almost equal throughout the English counties but, passing from East to West across southern England, the **B:C** ratio steadily increases to 1.43 : 1 in Devon (and 2:1 in Cornwall). These ratios do not reflect recent devastation, unpopulated estates, or superior agricultural methods requiring less oxen or more-fertile soils. Rather, Maitland (1897, p. 490) claimed such

> figures seem to show that men were sparse and poor; also they were servile. We suspect their tillage to have been that backward kind which ploughs enormous tracts for a poor return.

The number of tenants and occupiers recorded in Devon by Domesday was 17,434, though multiplication by four to six is needed to estimate the actual population. The ratio of recorded population to number of teamlands (**B** above) never fell to 2.0 in England, and only twice exceeded 4.0; however, in Devon the ratio is only 2.1. Devon and Cornwall are at the bottom in terms of the number of households that an average teamland supported.

Probably only a third to two-thirds of land that was sometimes ploughed in Devon was actually sowed in any one year, and husbandry differed radically from that in the fields of eastern England because of the topography and soils. Also, mensuration systems appropriate to open fields in the east were probably extremely inaccurate for the Celtic agriculture of Cornubia, so the Domesday reporters may have had to rely on significant guesswork in the southwest (Maitland, 1897, pp. 490-1).

Eight castrated oxen for a ploughing team, despite having perhaps a dozen years of useful service, imply a considerable herd of cattle to maintain a viable team, including a bull and numerous cows and followers. It is more difficult to interpret Domesday sheep and pig animal numbers with certainty. When Exon. Domesday recorded swine (porcos), sheep (oues), and head of cattle (animalia), porcus femina or ovis femina were not used; the small numbers of pigs recorded may reflect males only, implying additional numbers of sows and young.

WIDECOMBE-IN-THE-MOOR IN THE DOMESDAY BOOK

Some manorial identities within what is now the Parish of Widecombe-in-the-Moor have remained broadly unchanged for over 900 years since the Norman Conquest in 1066, and possibly for many years before that. At the end of the 19th century, nearly 44% of the land comprising the six manors in Widecombe-in-the-Moor Parish was common land.

As mentioned above, English counties were divided into hundreds for legal and administrative purposes. The Late Saxon Devon hundreds were shown in Thorn and Thorn's (1985, Part 2) and Turner's (2006, Fig 7) maps (see Fig. 9). Although their names evolved, the difference between boundaries in 1083 and later times was not great. Kerswell (Carsuella) Hundred, taxed for 50 hides in 1083, became Haytor Hundred with a detached moorland portion, which may have originated as moorland pasture that was an outlying part of the main hundred (just as Dewdon, Jordan, was a member of Cockington Manor near Torquay). The detached portion of Haytor Hundred now comprises Widecombe-in-the-Moor and Buckland-in-the-Moor. Various spellings for this hundred are found in the 1083 Geld Inquest of the Exon. Domesday, *viz*:

Modern	Haytor
Exon. Domesday list I	Cersuuelle
Exon. Domesday list II	Carsuelle
Exon. Domesday list III	Carsewilla (Kerswell) 50 hides

Figure 7 shows the approximate boundaries of Widecombe-in-the-Moor's seven current manors; the 20th century landscape is reflected by the Ordnance Survey Popular Edition map of 1919 (see Fig. 8). Although difficult to recapture much about the life and culture, it is useful to examine what Domesday recorded about the manors in what is now Widecombe-in-the-Moor. Following its translation from Latin, the Devonshire Association for the Advancement of Science, Literature, and Art decided in January 1884 to publish that part of Domesday relating to Devon (Devon. Assoc., 1884-1892). The Association's seven-member committee for this task included Robert Dymond, Lord of Dunstone Manor, Widecombe-in-the-Moor, who died before the two-volume work was completed. In his *Things New and Old* (Dymond, 1876), he had claimed that five of the six modern-day Widecombe manors were recorded in Domesday Book. However, recent studies show that only three of those five Domesday manors were in Widecombe-in-the-Moor. Lineham (1962) later identified Jordan as the Deptona manor in Domesday. Although legitimate controversy continues, following Thorn and Thorn's (1985) detailed analyses, the only Widecombe manors recorded in the Domesday Book appear to be:

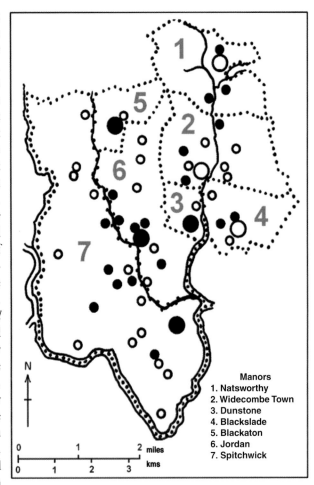

Figure 7. Sketch map of the current manor boundaries in Widecombe-in-the-Moor Parish. Solid black circles are single farms, small open circles hamlets, and large open circles manors (or manor sites). Adapted from Gawne (1970, p. 50, Fig. 1).

Present day		recorded as	
Spitchwick			Espicewita
Dunstone			Dunestanetuna with Blachestac added
Natsworthy			Noteswrde
Jordan			Depdona

29

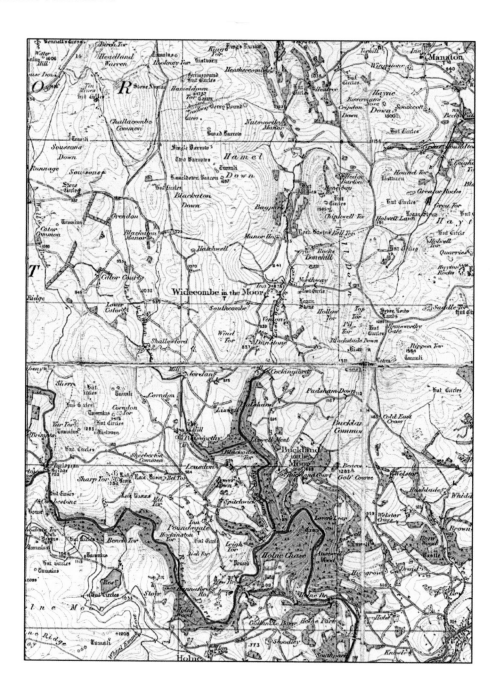

Figure 8. Area around Widecombe-in-the-Moor and Bonehill, Devon, in the early 20th century as shown in the 1:63,360 Ordnance Survey Popular Edition One-Inch Map Sheet 138 [*Contoured road map of Dartmoor and Exeter*] printed in 1919. The grid lines (True N-S and E-W) are 2 miles (3.219 km) apart. Original map sold mounted on linen and folded.

The Domesday record also included a tenement within the Parish of Widecombe-in-the-Moor (see Devon. Assoc., 1884-92, p. 130; Thorn and Thorn, 1985, Part 2, 3,8) - present day Scobitor, recorded as Scabatora (Scabatoe), the abode of two thegns belonging to the manor of Bovi (Bovey). Of these five properties, Natsworthy is recorded only in the later Exchequer Domesday Book (Exch.), while the other four are also detailed in the Exeter Domesday (Exon.).

Spitchwick Manor

(Espicewita - Exon.; Spicewite – Exch.; Devon. Assoc., 1884-92, pp. 66-7).

At the end of the 19th century, this manor was three times the area of Widecombe Town Manor, comprising 4,780 acres (1,936 ha) including a little over 2,215 acres (897 ha) of commons; the areas of Poundsgate, Lower Town (formerly Christianhayes), and Ponsworthy were included (Dymond, 1876, p. 22). The manor may have had somewhat different boundaries in 1086. According to Domesday, Espicwita was *Terra Regis*, or an estate which King William I held, having not bestowed it on any of his subjects. Domesday stated that Earl Harold had held the manor on the day on which King Edward was alive and dead (*i.e.*, on 5th January, 1066). Although Harold was King of England from 6th January to 14th October, 1066, William had not recognised his title to the crown; hence, use of Earl Harold in Domesday. Harold had paid land tax (geld) for only one hide, suggesting he held the large manor as a privilege at nominal tax. In fact, the manor must have been a flourishing estate, having land for 8 ploughs (nominally some 960 acres of arable) in manor demesne (*i.e.*, in lordship), and the villagers apparently had half a hide and four ploughs (probably $4\frac{1}{2}$ hides in all). There were eight villagers (bondsmen), four small-holders (bordars), and five slaves recorded. The estate included woodland extending to some $1\frac{1}{2}$ by $\frac{1}{8}$ mile (one league by one furlong) and 100 acres of pasture land [Thorn and Thorn, 1985, Part 2, 1,48].

Dunstone Manor and appendant Blackslade Estate

(Dunestanetuna & Blachestac – Exon.; Dunestantune & Blachestach – Exch.; Devon. Assoc., 1884-92, pp. 954-5).

This was one of Ralph of Pomeroy's estates (given to him by William the Conqueror) which later formed the Honour of Berry (named from Berry Pomeroy, Haytor Hundred). Edwin held the estate in the time of King Edward while, in 1086, Roger held it from Ralph, paying land tax for half a virgate of land ($\frac{1}{8}$ hide, or about 15 acres of arable) for Dunstone and one virgate for Blackslade, although each manor had land for one plough (120 acres each). At Dunstone Manor, Roger had three villeins (bondsmen tenants) and four small-holders (bordars) who had half a plough, five head of cattle, and three sheep. There were three acres of meadow and 30 acres of pasture. The manor was valued at 7*s.*6*d.* per annum in

1086, but was worth only 30*d.* when Roger acquired it. Blackslade was recorded as having two villeins (villagers) and three small-holders (bordars), two acres of meadow and a value of 3*s.* per annum. Dunstone and Blackslade were bought at auction by Robert Dymond in 1869 and then comprised 933 acres (377 ha), including 400 acres (162 ha) of commons (Dymond, 1876, p. 40). Thorn and Thorn (1985, Part 2, 34,46) suggested that, if Blackslade [Blachestac] (or Dunstone and Blackslade – their wording is ambiguous) "..is later represented by *Withecumb'* [Widecombe-in-the-Moor], held by Richard son of Ralph ..., then the overlordship early passed to the Honour of Plympton" (*cf.,* Reichel, 1908, p.124); this may imply Widecombe-in-the-Moor was an offshoot of this manor.

Natsworthy Manor

(Noteswrde – Exch.; Devon. Assoc., 1884-92, p. 893).

At the end of the 19th century, this manor comprised some 1,400 acres (567 ha) of which 605 (245 ha) were commons. Richard, son of Thorold (a vassal of the powerful Earl of Mortain), held the manor directly from King William, while Edward had held it before 1066, paying geld for one furlong. Domesday recorded land for two ploughs, one slave (serf), two villagers (villeins), and two small-holders (bordars). Meadows extended to five and coppice (underwood) to six acres, being worth 15*s.* per annum in 1086; the estate was formerly worth 5*s.* This is the highest manor recorded on Dartmoor. Lineham (1962, p. 468) stated "... the Hamlyns of Widecombe obtained their first property in the parish by barter with Richard son of Turold, who held Natsworthy under the earl .... about the same time (1187 to 1200)"; these dates seem to imply an extra layer of lordship/homage since Richard held the estate in 1086.

Jordan Manor

(Depdona - Exon.; Deptone – Exch., Devon. Assoc., 1884-92, pp. 732-3).

Lineham (1962) provided a detailed account of this manor which, according to the Tithe award in 1844, extended to 1,260 acres (510 ha); Dymond (1876, p. 1) listed 393 acres (159 ha) of common. The name Deptone may have been derived from an original Dewdone, meaning dewy upland in Old English; the name Dewdon survived until at least 1737 (Gover, *et al.,* 1932, ii, p. 527) before becoming Jordan. In 1086, Deptone was an outlying part of Cockington, a manor William of Falaise held from King William, Falaise being in the French department of Calvados. Alric (apparently a Saxon) held Deptone which was assessed as one virgate for land tax; probably he had held the land before the King gave it to William of Falaise. Its value was 10*s.* per annum in 1086. Lineham (1962, p. 467), after calculating the land unaccounted for at Cockington in Domesday, suggested Deptone had land for one plough or 64 acres.

Scobitor

(Scabatora - Exon.; Scabatore - Exch.; 1884-92, pp. 130-1).

In Domesday, this small estate is recorded as a remote outlier of Bovey Tracey Manor comprising bookland (*i.e.*, land taken from the common land and added to the manor and granted by charter to private owners). Two thanes occupied Scobitor and paid several shillings annually to Bovey Tracey Manor; these thanes, along with thirteen others in similar booklands, had held their lands jointly before 1066 and were " ... so free that they could go with their lands to whichever lord they would in 1066." In 1086, Bovey Tracey Manor was held by Geoffrey Mowbray, who had been consecrated Bishop of Coutances in 1048 or 1049; he had arrived in England in 1066, was chief chaplain at the Battle of Hastings, and played an important part in William's consecration as King at Westminster. He was rewarded with many lands in England which formed his personal fief, rather than that of the Church of Coutances (Thorn and Thorn, 1985, Part 2, 3,8).

Problems remain unresolved about two other current Widecombe-in-the-Moor manors, *viz*:

Blackaton, or Blagdon-Pipard, Manor

Dymond (1876, p. 36) wrote that this smallest manor in the parish contained about 600 acres (243 ha), of which half were uncultivated common. He suggested that "... [a]lthough clear proof is wanting, there are grounds for the assumption..." that this is Bachedona manor of Domesday. However, Thorn and Thorn (1985, Part 2, 17/34) identified Bachedon as Bagton in West Alvington Parish (Stanborough Hundred); if they are correct, this means Blackaton manor was not named in Domesday and must either have been omitted, included under another name, or be a post-Domesday acquisition, although it was an Okehampton Honour holding, which Baldwin the Sheriff's estates became at a later date (Thorn and Thorn, 1985, Part 2, 16; 16,163). Dymond (1876, p. 37) noted that Rolls of Letters Patent in 1214 show that King John granted William the Pipard lands at Baketon, etc., which were previously owned by William de la Ferbe; it is questionable whether Baketon was indeed Blackaton and whether the latter was a manor in 1086. Over the past few hundred years, Blagdon-Pipard (very variously spelled) appeared frequently in legal documents but, in the recent past, Blackaton has been the commonly used name.

Widecombe (Widecombe Town) Manor

Dymond (1876, p. 32) cited the current area as about 1,575 acres (638 ha), including 706 acres (286 ha) of commons, the church and village, the glebe, Northall, Southcombe, Wooda (Woodhayes), Kingshead, Coombe, Northway, Southway, and Scobetor. He concluded that it "... seems more probable that the manor ... may be recognised [as] ... an estate with a house called Wodiacoma", as Risdon (1811, p. 151) had claimed almost 250 years previously.

However, Thorn and Thorn (1985, Part 2, 23/24) concluded that Wodiacome was really ?Woodcombe, claiming that

> the order of Exon. places it clearly in Chillington (Coleridge) Hundred ...; it may well be the place in Chivelstone parish, although neither this place nor the entries for Coleridge ... are found in fee lists ... The DB [Exchequer Domesday] form points rather to Woodcombe

which is near Start Point. Thorn and Thorn's (1985, Part 2, 34,46) enigmatic allusion to *Withecumb'* (cited above) is the only allusion to Widecombe-in-the-Moor Manor in their monumental study, which implies that Widecombe Manor was not explicitly mentioned in Domesday.

Northall Manor, in the village centre, was built in post-Domesday times (see Chapter 2).

Other possible manors

At least three other Domesday estates have been interpreted as having been in what is now Widecombe-in-the-Moor Parish. Although some uncertainties remain, recent research attributes them all to other regions. Darby and Versey (1975) suggested the small Haiserstona Domesday manor (Devon. Assoc., 1884-92, pp. 254-5) was present-day Sherbaton, and Beeson and Materman (19789, p.60) accepted this; however, Thorn and Thorn (1985, Part 2, 6,6) seem correct in following Gover, *et al.* (1932, p. 487), who identified it as Ashton Parish (far away in Exminister Hundred). Again, Lega and Suetetona (Devon. Assoc., 1884-92, pp. 1056-7) believed to be Leigh and Sweaton by Worth (1892) are now thought to have been estates in Halberton Hundred (Thorn and Thorn, 1985, Part 2, 41,1 & 41,2).

Ewes at Lower Bonehill in the Spring.

2

THE REGION ABOUT BONEHILL AND WIDECOMBE

1086 TO THE MID-17TH CENTURY

Direct evidence about Bonehill and Widecombe-in-the-Moor between 1086 and the mid-17th century is scarce, so what living conditions and communication were really like on this part of Dartmoor in the years following the Norman Conquest still remain somewhat obscure. However, by examining the evolution of the immediate area and the changing lordship until the mid-17th century, the ambience of the hamlet can begin to be pictured. Before the end of this period, Bonehill had become one of the important and elegant hamlets in the Parish of Widecombe-in-the-Moor, with fine new granite longhouses and supporting outbuildings, plus a substantial community ranging from yeomen to numerous labourers and servants. The mid-17th century is wholly arbitrary as the end date for this Chapter, except that very complex changes in the Lordship of the Manor of Widecombe-in-the-Moor (and several adjacent manors) occurred within a decade or so each side of 1700, which are explained in Chapter 3. The ramifications of these changes had a major affect on the leases and ownership of the Bonehill and Widecombe tenements (see Chapter 4).

In the beginning

A well-known figure in Widecombe, the late Miss Elizabeth Gawne (1970, p. 49), wrote:

> The upper valley of the River Dart is larger and wider than the other river valleys of Dartmoor, and penetrates much farther into the centre of the uplands. It is almost entirely occupied by the Parish of Widecombe, and by the part of the parish of Lydford which contains the Ancient Tenements of the Forest of Dartmoor. Widecombe is the only parish which is entirely within the Moor, and was the last reached by the higher tides of land hunger, and the first to abandon its marginal fields when the pressure subsided. Many layers of deserted banks and boundaries can be seen on the hillsides, and their basic pattern can be followed in the shapes of the cultivated fields below.

The sparsity of data was well illustrated by Turner's (2006) study of the evolving Christian landscape in the southwest, which included a useful map of the Late Saxon hundreds (adapted from Thorn & Thorn, 1985, vol. 2) and the important Devon churches of the 5th to mid-11th centuries (his early-medieval period). The nearest churches to Widecombe were at Buckfast, Tavistock, and Exeter (see Fig. 9). His (Turner, 2006, Fig. 49) map of east Devon showed that all royal-estate centres mentioned in Domesday were in valley bottoms, while the smaller manors (less than five hides) were in the surrounding hills. He (2006, pp. 186-8) suggested that almost

> all high-status churches in the South West lay at the heart of major agricultural estates which were either held directly by the ecclesiastical community itself or were associated with royal estate centres located nearby. ... As more and more land was reclaimed from the rough ground or woodland and granted to thegns between the ninth and eleventh centuries, the number and size of ... [minor] estates increased, placing increasing pressure on the core areas of settlement.

Turner concluded that each major ecclesiastical centre was an important focus for spiritual, political, and economic life, and thus a powerful influence on the imaginations of people living in the area.

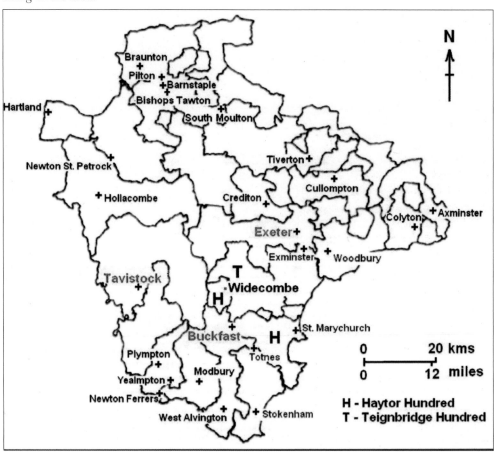

Figure 9. – Late Saxon Hundred boundaries in Devon; H = Haytor Hundred; T = Teignbridge Hundred. All important early medieval churches (+) identified by Turner (2006) are named; the nearest three to Widecombe are shown in red. Present-day Widecombe, in the small separated part of Haytor Hundred, is identified by the red dot and name (Widecombe). Adapted from Turner, 2006, Fig. 7.

By the 11th century, colonisation of land over 1,000 feet (305 m) seems to have been undertaken for a while; surprisingly, with the earlier stone houses and abundant granite boulders lying around in many areas, the Saxon tradition of building with wood persisted. Beneath the ruined stone-walled houses of the medieval village preserved at 1,200 feet (366 m) near Hound Tor, some two miles (3.2 km) northeast of Widecombe, there is evidence of wattle and turf huts having been rebuilt repeatedly on almost identical sites (Cocks, 1970, p. 79). The higher parts of Dartmoor may well have been significantly more deprived and primitive during the medieval periods than the more accessible lowland areas of Devon (which feature in most preserved records). It is not unlikely that a wooden Saxon church occupied the present site of Widecombe's St. Pancras church. Hemery (1983, p. 607) seems correct in believing that considerable human movement into and out from the moors around Widecombe was occurring

> before the Norman Conquest, for in the combes of the eastern highlands men lived in houses of wood and stone and farmed the land as serfs under the Saxon manor lords largely undisturbed...

Despite the four manors and a tenement identified in Domesday Book within what is now the Parish of Widecombe-in-the-Moor, no manorial estates were recorded in the East Webburn River valley, where the village focus around the church developed soon after Domesday Book times.

Around manor houses and farmsteads in the hilly parts of Devon, a limited area (the infield) was usually under permanent cultivation in a rotation of crops; the larger outfield beyond was cultivated for several successive years and then let down to rough grazing before being returned to cultivation again. According to Hoskins, population pressure across Devon accompanying colonisation between 1150 and 1350 led to many new farms being established with small enclosed fields; increasing amounts of outfield land was also appropriated by individuals for more intensive cultivation. Hoskins (1954, p. 58) suggested that nearly all the colonisation of moorland was by free peasants, who held a charter from a lord of the manor that defined a specific piece of land.

The only Devon monastic houses recorded in Domesday were the Benedictine abbeys of Tavistock (founded 974) and Buckfast (founded 1030), although several others had been established by the end of the 11th century. Around Exeter, as in the rest of England, significant religious revival occurred in the 12th and 13th centuries, with parish churches being rebuilt in stone throughout the Exeter Diocese. Exeter was the fourth largest English diocese in medieval times.

A significant church definitely existed at Widecombe-in-the-Moor well before 1260. The rector of Widecombe parish church is mentioned in Bishop Walter Bronescombe's Register dated in Crediton 20th August, 1260; this Latin document (Exeter Episcopal Registers, Folio 16, b) was reproduced in full by Rowe (1896, pp. 291-2). Bishop Bronescombe apparently summoned the rectors of Lydford and Widecombe following receipt of a certificate from the Archdeacon of Totnes that inhabitants of the villages of Babbeneye [Babeny] and Pushyle [Pushill] were unable to 'erect a house of prayer', and Widecombe parish church was their nearest church (Dymond, 1876, p. 16). In good summer weather, Lydford was eight miles (12.9 km) across the Moor from these villages but detours due to boggy mires and swollen rivers in bad weather increased the walk to 15 miles (24.1 km). The bishop ordained that, henceforth, while remaining parishoners of the Lydford mother church, Babeny and Pushill residents should hear divine service and receive the sacraments at Widecombe and contribute (with the parishoners of Widecombe) to the repair and building of that church and to the enclosing of its churchyard although, in token of subjection and parochial rights, they were to pay all tithes (except that of lambs) to Lydford.

Before 1283, a substantial North Hall manor house existed, just north of the present Widecombe-in-the-Moor Green. Worthy (1874) and later Dymond (1876, pp. 14-6, 33) referred to their having examined three documents in Chapter Archives in the Exchequer room over St. Andrew's Chapel at Exeter Cathedral. Their reports differ in a few details, which may reflect differing understanding of the original Latin, but they agreed that:

(**a**) The first document, a deed, showed that Sir Ralph le Rous (of an ancient Modbury family, the Ralphs or Fitz-Ralphs), who is the earliest *recorded* lord of the North Hall Manor, Widecombe, had sold an acre (0.4 ha) of land to his son Roger. Roger le Rous gave (according to Worthy) or sold (according to Dymond) this acre at Wydecomb, with the advowson of the Church of St. Pancras, to the Dean and Chapter of Exeter. Worthy (1874) wrote that the deed reported the acre

" ... lies in Wodehaye, near the sanctuary of the aforesaid Church, and extends in length from the aforesaid sanctuary, from the western part, up to the high road, through which it goes, from the aforesaid Church of Wydecombe, towards Dunsterston, from the eastern part." *Que quidem acra terre jacet in Wodehaye prope sanctuarium ecclesiæ superadictæ, et extendit in longtudine a predicto sanctuario ex-parte occidentali usque ad regalem viam per quam itur a dicta ecclesia de Wydecombe versus Duntorston ex-parte orientali.*

Dymond (1876, p. 15) used slightly different wording, writing that the acre was

adjacent to the mother church of the parish ... lying in Wodehaye [now Wooda or Wooder] hard by the sanctuary of the church, and extending lengthwise from the west part of the said sanctuary as far eastward as the highway leading from the church towards Dunsterton [Dunstone].

Both authors agree Roger's transfer of the acre was in perpetuity, subject to the Dean and Chapter

(**i**) rendering annually to the lord of Widecombe manor - presumably the Lord of North Hall Manor - at Michaelmas a pair of candlesticks, or one penny for all secular service, as enumerated in the Deed by which Roger had been granted the land by the lord of the manor, Sir Ralph (a son of Sir Richard), and

(**ii**) paying 10 silver marks annually for the performance of divine service in their

Cathedral in good memory of Dean Roger de Thoriz, who died on 29th April, 1274. (This service was apparently conducted until the Reformation, when the cathedral "devised for a superstitious use" fell by the Statute of Chantries to the Crown in Edward VI's reign, until the Restoration under Queen Elizabeth I.)

(b) The second document (dated the Saturday before the Purification of the blessed Mary, 1283) was Bishop Quivil's appropriation of the advowson by the institution of John, son of Richard, as vicar of Widecombe Parish and providing for the masses for Dean Roger de Thoriz to be said at the altar of Saints Richard and Radigund, near Exeter Cathedral's west door.

(c) The third document, a bond, dated the Saturday before the Feast of the Nativity of the Blessed Mary (? September) 1283, recorded the earlier sale of the acre and the advowson by Sir Ralph, manorial lord of North Hall, to his son Roger le Rous. Dymond (1876, p. 15) wrote that the Bond

> by Ralph, the son of Sir Richard and Roger le Rous, rector (sic) of the Church of Nordhull [North Hall, the Manor House], ...

showed the sale was for 80 marks plus a further 20 marks for Sir Ralph's daughter's dowry; thirty marks had already been paid by Roger le Rous and the remainder was to be paid in instalments. Dymond seems to have recognised the possible anomaly here by including "(sic)". Since this bond was dated after the sale earlier in 1283, it was important in recording the ongoing debt of 50 plus 20 marks; also, it is possible that Roger le Rous was rector of a chapel at North Hall manor, while John was vicar of the Widecombe parish church. Dymond's writing about these late 13th century events is very convoluted (*cf.*, Worthy, 1875); further recourse to the original Latin documents might be helpful. Dymond's (1876, p. 21) compilation of Widecombe vicars did not extend back into the 13th century.

Although Dymond interpreted Wodehaye as being either Wooda or Wooder (see above), the old church is likely to have been on the site of the present-day granite Parish Church of St. Pancras in the centre of Widecombe-in-the-Moor village (*cf.*, Cresswell, 1932, p. 23, who alluded to the original 'church of North Hall'). The raised ground about the present-church site has caused some to speculate on whether there may have been an earlier Saxon wooden church on this site. Recent fieldwork showed North Hall Manor house was just north of the present Village Green (Rennells, 1999; Widecombe History Group, 2000). Rennells (2008a) reported that archaeological evidence is beginning to suggest North Hall was a *ca.* 13th century stronghold (surrounded by a moat) of a style unusual in Devon; it appears to have comprised several buildings. A decade ago, the late Ned Northmore (*pers. cmmn*) asserted firmly that he had seen water standing in the remains of North Hall moat in really wet winters.

The Village Green used to be known as Henhay, *alias* Butte Park, which Dymond (1876, p. 57) believed was provided for use by parish inhabitants in obedience to the 1466 Act of Parliament requiring that:

> every Englishman should have a bow of his own height of yew, ash, wych, hazel, or amburn; and that butts should be made in every township, which the inhabitants were to shoot at every feast-day under penalty of a halfpenny when they should omit that exercise.

The old name of Butte Park presumably referred to there formerly having been butts for the protection of those standing behind the archery targets.

Dymond's reference to a 'highway' leading to Dunsterton from Widecombe in 1283 could be misleading today, because permanent routeways are unlikely to have been of any importance until the earliest towns of Lydford, Tavistock, and Okehampton began to develop adjacent to Dartmoor except, possibly, for routes flanking the north and west of Dartmoor. Travellers on Dartmoor had to go by foot or horse-back. Crossing rivers was a major problem (especially in times of flood) and resulted in granite bridges being built on a few major routeways by the 13th century (*e.g*, Great Bridge across the River Tavy near Tavistock in about 1260, and the Holne Bridges across the River Dart, which were re-built in 1413. The building dates of most of the old Devon bridges were cited by Bennett (2007, p. 42).

Although farming was progressively encroaching on the edges of Devon's moorland in the 12th century and, by the early 14th century, settlements were multiplying on Dartmoor, Hoskins showed that the population of Devon was then almost the same as in 1086 (on the basis of the 1377 Poll Tax returns of all people over the age of 14). This was the smallest change in population density amongst all English counties, despite Devon's population having reached a peak of some 109,300 in 1347-8. Over the same period, Cornwall's population density rose from 14th to 37th, the highest in the country. Across the whole region between 1314 and 1322 there was a period of severe harvest failures and disastrous cattle and sheep epidemics, due to several years of severe wet conditions; the loss of oxen impacted arable cultivation badly. Moore's (1890) estimate that, in 1345, more than 90% of holdings on Dartmoor were 10 acres or larger has often been quoted, but productivity of much of this land was generally low. Miller and Hatcher (1978, p. 250) made a detailed survey of the life and generally protein-deficient diet of rural English peasantry during these difficult years, concluding that, across the country, the plague caused

> a radical break in what otherwise might have been an evolutionary trend. ... Plague mortality ... raised once more the wages of labourers and increased still further the availability of land to tenants, augmenting yet again the purchasing power of the mass market.

So, living conditions were far from easy and there was a disproportionate rise in mortality among the village poor in the famine years of the early 14th century. It seems probable that the ravages of successive Black Death epidemics across England as a whole from 1340 onwards were more severe in Devon than elsewhere, even in the open country and, as a result, much land became unoccupied as the population declined. It is difficult to tell how the high Moors residents fared in comparison with the general rural population assessed in the literature; only scraps of data relating specifically to the Widecombe area have been unearthed. Hoskins (1954, pp. 169-70) concluded that:

> Even on Dartmoor the effects were felt. The bailiff's account for Dartmoor manor in 1350-1 gives a long list of the moorland farms "in the hands of the lord for want of tenants," and we find that as late as 1355 no tin was being produced on the moor. The output from Devon that year was nil.

Havinden and Wilkinson (1970, p. 148) cited Moore's (1890) list of Dartmoor tenants in 1345 which showed the number of tenants (44) and the land under cultivation (23 ferlings) had both almost doubled over 45 years; however, they suggested that some of these tenants may have merely held small pieces of land while living some distance away.

Devon recovered quickly from the bubonic plague, with considerable re-building of parish churches, bridges, and manor houses in the late 14th century. Details of the development and ownership of Widecombe-area estates over the centuries may always remain a little obscure, but preserved historical evidence shows it was sometimes complex.

Buckfast Abbey had been re-founded in 1136. Englebourne (Inglebourne in Risdon, Worthy, and Dymond), in the parish of Harberton, had belonged to the Benedictine Abbey in Buckfastleigh, having been granted to the Abbot in 1244, apparently by the gift of Peter, son of Matthew of Stoke in the Hamme (Risdon, 1811, pp. 165-6; Thorn and Thorn, 1985, Part 2, 1,24, 1,34, & 16,175). Englebourne, some 5½ miles (ca. 9 km) southeast of the Abbey, is mentioned frequently below, after its acquisition by the Wotton family.

To follow Dymond (1876, pp. 33-5), it seems that, after King Edward I's time (i.e., after 1307), the Fitz-Ralphs took the name de Shillingford (from the family's connection with the Parish of Shillingford St. George, near Exeter). The inquisition following Thomas Shillingford's death in 1311, recorded he had held 'Wydecumb hamlet extent'. Baldwin de Shillingford bequeathed his family property to his apparently illegitimate son, John Shillingford; the inquisition following the latter's death in 1461 showed he had held land, tenements, and rents in "Wydecomb in the More". John's son William sold these properties (which included North Hall and other parts of Widecombe) in about 1470-80 to William Huddlesfield, who was Recorder of Exeter (1479-82), Attorney General under Richard II, knighted by Henry VII, and died 1499.

Sir William Huddersfield had no male heir, but his second daughter Elizabeth married Sir Anthony Pointz (of Acton, Gloucestershire) and she sold both the Shillingford and Widecombe properties to John Southcote (born - 1510/11; died - 1585), who built a substantial house at Indio, Bovey Tracey, obtaining a permanent lease for that property in 1531. Reflecting his purchase of the Widecombe estates, it is found that in 1545, John Southcote, lord of Widecombe, granted a 99-year lease for a tenement in Natsworthy to Adam Drewe and his wife Mary (DRO 48/14/50/12).

The tin trade grew rapidly and reached a peak in 1515, remaining almost as strong for a decade or so before declining through the 16th century. Around Widecombe, tin ore was extracted both from the extensive alluvial gravels and from adits and shallow mines; after smelting locally, the tin ingots were transported to, and sold at, Ashburton, which is well known as an important stannery town. The parish guild of St. Pancras of Widecombe either received gifts of tin or invested funds in local tin workings; it appeared in the Coinage Roll of 1523, together with the names of several Widecombe men (Hoskins, 1954, p. 542). Official subsidy data collected for 1524 reflected a significant growth of the wage-earning property-less labouring class in Devon – a group that comprised a third of the population in the deep countryside (Hoskins, 1954, p. 64).

At the dissolution of the monasteries under King Henry VIII in 1536-9, Buckfast Abbey properties included two tenements in Spitchwick, Widecombe Parish, yielding annual rents of £1.14s.8d. (Dymond, 1876, p. 25 citing *Valor Ecclesiaticus empt. Henrici VIII*). It is unknown how much of Dartmoor had been within the enormous estates of the Courtenays, other important families, and the ecclesiastical authorities. Hoskins (1954, p. 83) concluded that Devon property which

> fell into the hands of the Crown in 1536-9 was well over £6,700 a year, the equivalent of about five times the extent of the great Courtenay domain in Devon ... which [itself] was in the hands of the Crown by 1536. The changes which took place in Devon as a result of the disposal of most of these lands [was] the greatest transference of property since the Norman Conquest.

According to Worthy (1874; 1875, pp. 61-2), the Wotton family purchased Englebourne (a portion of the sequestered possessions of Buckfast Abbey) from the Crown on 21st September, 1546.

Hoskins (1954, p. 170) wrote that

> muster-books of able-bodied men between 1558 and 1588 reveal that Devon was now the second or third most populous county in England ... the rise of Devon from one of the most thinly and under-populated counties in 1377 to one of the most densely peopled in Elizabethan days is unmistakable. Not all this tremendous increase could have been natural: immigration from other counties and from across the Irish and English Channels undoubtedly played a large part.

On the basis of various 16th century surveys preserved in the Public Record Office, he (p. 90) also concluded that, of 24 rural Devon manors with a total of 1,241 tenants, *free* tenants had risen significantly to comprise about 20% of rural tenantry by the mid-16th century. *Customary* tenants (the copyholders), holding their land according to the custom of the manor by copy of the manor court roll, comprised 75% of the manorial tenants; the number of leaseholders (*conventionary* tenants) increased in a few manors. Unhappily, it is unknown how closely tenantry in manors and land holdings around Widecombe-in-the-Moor corresponded to the county averages.

The present Widecombe-in-the-Moor church was probably rebuilt late in the 15th century; according to Dymond (1876, p. 113), the fine tower "was erected, it is said, by tin-streamers of the 15th or 16th century, as a thankoffering to GOD for their success in the neighbour-hood." It might have been hoped that the orientation of St. Pancras church could yield clues about its initial building date. Muirden's (2005) careful study of Devon church orientations showed their alignment has a scatter of 20 degrees or more, with a mean of some five or six degrees north of east (true bearings, as distinct from degrees from magnetic north); as he pointed out, numerous studies have shown that considerably more English churches are aligned to the left of east, than directly towards true east. Although Widecombe church was not included in his study, Muirden (2006, *pers. commn*) later determined St. Pancras has an 'adopted alignment' of 93½ degrees east of north. Muirden always gave particular attention to the orientation of the chancel east wall, because they ".. probably marked the most sanctified part of the church (adjacent to the altar), and is least likely to have undergone later upheaval..."; unlike many churches, different parts of St. Pancras vary from the adopted alignment by only one or two degrees.

Dietz (2005, p.1) asserted that:

> by the sixth century, the sanctuary within the church was regularly placed at the east end, the direction which throughout history has symbolized the eschaton: the second coming of Christ in kingly glory. The ancient custom of orienting churches alludes not only to Matthew 24.27, "As the lightening cometh out from the east ... so also will the coming of the Son of Man be," but more importantly to the direction the Jewish high priest faced in the Jerusalem Temple when offering sacrifice on Yom Kippur, the "day of atonement," the most important and essential feast of the Jewish year.

Although tempting to seek an interesting story in the variation of church orientations in Devon and England generally (*cf*, Muirden, 2005), none of the many possible and varied explanations seems convincing. Alignment with the patronal sunrise has been suggested for some churches, but the orientation of St Pancras to the south of east is currently unexplained. Until it can be determined whether or not early church builders had striven to achieve a precise easterly alignment (as many architects in prehistoric times appear to have done), one should agree with Hinton (2004, p. 50) that it is only

> reasonable to conclude that churches were originally vaguely aligned eastwards, but that for some reason a more accurate orientation became increasingly important over time.

The main Lower and Middle Bonehill farmhouses date from the late mid-16th century; it is likely, though not certain, that John Southcote had them built. Brown's (1988a) genealogical research showed that a John Smerdon's children were born at 'Bonehill' early in 1570, but nothing is known about the Smerdon's social status at that time. It is shown later that, because Richard Cabell of Buckfastleigh owned Middle Bonehill in 1658, when Arthur Smerdon held a three-lives lease, it is probable that John Southcote had owned the property before he died in 1585.

Although Smerdon ownership of Middle Bonehill (possibly deeply mortgaged) and yeoman status in 1570 are just possible, it is more likely that the Smerdon's were customary tenants, holding the farmstead according to the custom of John Southcote's Widecombe manor (?North Hall). Because a later John Smerdon of Bonehill was cited as yeoman in two 1733 independent legal documents, his predecessors possibly also had yeoman status. As already mentioned, Hoskins (1954) noted that, in Elizabethan and early Stuart times, customary tenants far outnumbered freeholders in Devon.

North Hall and John Southcote's other Widecombe properties were inherited by his eldest son, Thomas in 1585. In 1626, a Thomas Southcote granted a lease for North Hall Mansion, the barton lands and tenements, and three grist mills to Vincent Andrewe (miller) and his wife Margarett (DRO 48/14/47/1; cf., Rennells, 1999). Further leases in the Manors of Widecombe and Natsworthy were granted by Thomas Southcote, e.g., in 1638-9 (DRO 48/14/44/2 & 48/14/52/1).

The following poem about North Hall (a few meters north of Widecombe-in-the-Moor village green) written in iambic heptameter by Master Hill, schoolmaster of Widecombe in 1638, was quoted by both Dymond (1876, pp. 34-5) and Rowe (1896, p. 156):

> *The messuage there, which anciently was chief or capital,*
> *Tho' much decayed, remaining still is called yet North-hall:*
> *Whereas the houses, courtlages, with orchards, gardens, and*
> *A stately grove of trees within that place did sometime stand,*
> *Were all enclosed round about with moats of standing water,*
> *So that no thieves or enemies could enter in to batter.*
> *The houses, walls, roofs, windows, or what else besides was there;*
> *The moats or trenches being fed with streams of water clear,*
> *Wherein good store of fish was bred, as ancient men did say;*
> *The ruin'd banks whereof remain unto this very day.*
> *And when the family within would walk into the town,*
> *Or else return, a draw-bridge firm they presently let down:*
> *And at their pleasure drew it up to keep the household safe –*
> *This house did anciently belong to Ralph, the son of Ralph,*
> *So is he named in a deed of much antiquity,*
> *Which bears no date, for at that time was less iniquity.*

Despite Hill's reference to 'decayed' North Hall, Rennells (1999, 2008b) assiduous research over the past decade showed a series of families leased and occupied North Hall from 1626 until 1834, although he cited a *Daily Western Times* report about an excursion to see the ruins of North Hall in 1880. This may suggest Hill's decayed North Hall referred to the main stronghold, but that some of the ancillary buildings remained viable homesteads until the mid-19th century.

In settlement of Thomas and Sir Popham Southcote's debts, the Manors of "Blackdon Pyperd, Widdecombe, Trusham alias Trisme and Mannaton" were conveyed on 11th January, 1642, to Sir John Pole, Edmond Fortescue, and William Stowell for sale (DRO 48/14/7/1-2). It is unknown whether the debt (which must have been sizeable) resulted from problems associated with the imminent Civil War, business, gambling, or something else. The year 1642 was troubled, seeing the start of the first Civil War in England and then, on 19th July, issue of the Commission of Array for Devonshire to Henry Bourchier, Earl of Bath (then owner of Spitchwick) and 27 other leading figures in Devon, who were charged with organising royalist support across the county (*cf.*, Andriette, 1971, pp. 55, *et seq.*). Apparently, in 1646, the Indio estate, being close to the Civil War battlefield at nearby Heathfield, was a refuge for Royalist sympathisers.

The complex sequence of conveyances between 1650 and 1656 of what had been the Southcote's estates shows the intended sale (of 1642) was not effected, and the manors and other properties eventually became held in trust by John Merifield, esquire, of Crewkerne (Somerset) and Courtney Pole, esquire, of Exeter, for Sir John Pole, bart., of Colcombe (DRO 48/14/7/2–6). Table 1 is a guide to keeping the evolving ownership in perspective.

It is clear that, in addition to the Southcote holdings, other large tracts of what is now Widecombe-in-the-Moor had become owned by other powerful families. For example, Dymond (1876, p. 26) referred to a *post mortem* inquisition in 1434 by which Fulk Bourchier, Lord Fitzwarin, "... was declared to have been seized of the Manors of Spitchwick and St. Mary-Church...". In 1514, Sir John Bourgchier, Lord of Fitzwaren, provided a 60-year lease (DRO 48/14/40/3) for property which he obviously owned near Dartmeet, *viz*:

> An acre of land lying in the waste next to Dertameta, in the manor of Spechewyke, between the fountain there called Hangerwille on the south, and the water of Derta on the west, and Smethford on the north, and the way leading from Smethford as far as le Greneway on the east. Also a mill there called 'a blowyng myll and Knakkyng myll', with the weir and the stream of water flowing to the said mill, which [mill] Christopher and Richard lately built there.

In July, 1536, Henry VIII conferred the Earldom of Bath on Fulk's heir, John Bourchier, who, although born at Halstead (Essex) in 1470, was buried in Baunton (Devon) in April, 1539. John, Second Earl of Bath, sold all the trees growing in Spychwyke Parke to Robert Hamlyn, Richard Langworthy, and Thomas Hamlyn of Wythekon (*sic*) for £90 in January, 1542 (DRO 48/14/16/1), and all trees on Specheweke commons for £20 in 1590 (DRO 48/14/40/8a-b). Two tenements, four cottages, and a mill in his Spechewyke Manor were sold by the earl in 1544 for £58 (DRO 8/14/40/4). Numerous leases and other legal documents reflect continuing ownership of Spitchwick by the Earls of Bath into the 17th century (*e.g.*, DRO 48/14/16/2-8; 48/14/17/1-10; 48/14/26/2-9).

While most of the land and property was owned by powerful lords of the manors, the freehold to a few individual tenements in each manor were commonly owned by local farmers (often yeomen). For example, Latin Charters of Feoffment (essentially freehold) show lands, tenements, and rents within the demesne of Specheswyke (Spitchwick), inherited from his father Edward, were passed by John Baker to William Baker in 1433, and by William to Robert Baker in 1437 (DRO 48/14/40/1-2). In 1545, John Baker sold feoffment to that messuage and to Lake (DRO 48/14/21/1-2), and several documents record that the Bakers were involved with Spitchwick land transactions for at least another 40 years. A messuage was usually a dwelling house.

In addition to the Southcote family of Indio, Bovey Tracey, reference has been made to the Wotton's of Englebourne, Harberton (just southeast of Buckfastleigh). To follow the next phase of Widecombe's history, background about a third important Devon family, the Cabells of Brook(e) Manor, Buckfastleigh, will be helpful.

Although citing only some of her sources, which included Buckfastleigh graveyard, Mrs. S. Cabell Djabri (1991) unravelled the succession of Richard Cabells of the 17th century; they are labelled here 1, 2, 3,... for clarity (*cf.*, Sandles, 2007). Richard Cabell (1), MP, lived in Frome, Somerset, and died in 1584. His oldest son, Richard (2), moved to Devon and married a widow, Susannah Peter, from Buckfastleigh; he died in 1612, some 15 years after his wife. He had a son, Richard (3) who, after being educated at Exeter College (Oxford) and the Inns of Court, married the daughter of a wealthy Exeter merchant. Financially, Richard (3) was very successful; he extended the Cabell estates but, being a royalist, was subjected to crippling fines to keep Brook Manor during the Civil War, and he died on 24th August 1655. For perspective about the turbulent Civil War era, recall that King Charles I was executed in 1649 and Charles II was restored to the throne in 1660.

Richard (4), born in 1621, had his education at Oxford and the Middle Temple interrupted by the War; shortly after his father's death, he married Elizabeth Fowell in 1655. Elizabeth was a daughter of Sir Edward Fowell who had been President of the Committee of Sequestration in Devon which levied the wartime fines. The marriage seems to have enabled restoration of Cabell fortunes decimated by Civil War fines; it might be supposed that the fines had long been spent on Parliamentary causes – it is not recorded where money for the restoration came from. Anyway, renovation of Brook Manor, the Cabell family home, soon followed. If Djabri's and Sandles' reconstruction is correct, it must also have been Richard's (4) restored fortune that facilitated his purchase of numerous and extensive Widecombe properties from Sir Courtney Pole in 1658/9.

Marriage settlements in 1652 between members of the Cabell and Wotton families included extensive but scattered Devon properties (DRO 48/14/137/2a-b); these settlements must reflect close bonds between these affluent neighbouring Devon families. Later in 1652, Samuel and William Cabell secured legal title to extensive estates around Devon, including some in Widecombe (DRO 48/14/137/3). Also that year, Richard and Alice Mann enfe-offed by indentures (*i.e.*, transferred) a messuage at Stone (a tenement within the Manor of

Table 1
Summary of ownership and occupation in Widecombe-in-the-Moor to 1680

1030: The Benedictine Buckfast Abbey was founded (refounded 1136).

1260: A church existed in Widecombe-in-the-Moor before this.

1283: Sir Ralph le Rous recorded as Lord of Widecombe Manor by this date; the Ralphs, or Fitz-Ralphs, were of an ancient Modbury family.

1311: After 1307 Fitz-Ralphs took the name de Shillingford, and Thomas de Shillingford, who held Widecombe, died by 1311.

\-   : Baldwin de Shillingford's Widecombe estates passed to his illegitimate son, John Shillingford.

1461: John Shillingford died 1461, bequeathing North Hall and other Widecombe estates to his son, William Shillingford

1470-80: William Shillingford sold his Widecombe estates to Sir William Huddlesfield, who died in 1499.

1499: Elizabeth Huddlesfield inherited her father's Widecombe estates and later sold the Widecombe properties to John Southcote.

1539: Dissolution of monasteries by Henry VIII; Buckfast Abbey's properties appropriated by Crown included some Dartmoor estates (*e.g.*, at Spitchwick).

1545: John Southcote of Indio, Bovey Tracey, recorded as Lord of Widecombe; he died 1585.

1546: Many Devon estates bought from the Crown by the Wotton family of Englebourne, Harberton, Devon.

mid-16th century: Main Lower Bonehill (Bonneyhill) farmhouse built; shortly later, Middle Bonehill farmhouse built.

1570-2: John Smerdon's son Richard born at Bonehill.

1626: Thomas Southcote was granting major estate leases within Widecombe (possibly including Lower, but not Middle, Bonehill)

1642: Thomas Southcote's Widecombe properties, in settlement of a debt, conveyed for sale to Sir John Pole, Edmond Fortescue, and William Stowell, a sale which did not occur for some years.

1652: Richard (3) Cabell (of Brook Manor, Buckfastleigh) prospered and secured title to Devon estates (including some in Widecombe); as a royalist, he suffered severe fines during Civil War.

1655: Richard (3) Cabell died; soon thereafter son Richard (4) married Elizabeth Fowell, whose father secured restoration of Cabell fortunes to Richard (4).

1656: After complex sequence of conveyances and the Civil War, the Southcote's Widecombe properties became held in trust by John Merifield and Courtney Pole for Sir John Pole, bart.

1658: Richard (4) Cabell purchased Manors of Widecombe and Blagdon Pipard (Blackaton) and numerous other Widecombe properties (including what became the two Lower Bonehill farmsteads) from Sir Courtney Pole. Richard (4) became Lord of Manor of Widecombe.

1658: Arthur Smerdon in possession of on-going three-lives lease at Bonehill.

1677: Richard (4) Cabell died – his daughter Elizabeth (a minor) was executorix and inherited his estates (including the Manor of Widecombe); the Courts established administration during Elizabeth's minority.

1676-94: Samuel Cabell, possibly Richard's (3) brother, granted leases to many Widecombe properties – in 1682 he was described as lord of the premises of North Hall (Widecombe). Precise legal relationship between Elizabeth and Samuel Cabell unclear.

Natsworthy) to Richard Cabell (? 4) of the Middle Temple, London, esquire (DRO 48/14/51/3); the common of pasture in "Bunhildowne" (Bonehill Down) was included (DRO 48/14/51/4). Richard Mann's final conveyance of freehold (lease and release) to Richard Cabell (4) of Brook, esquire, was dated 1668 (DRO 14/51/5a-b). It was documented in 1652 that Richard (3), Samuel, and William Cabell were sons of Richard Cabell (2) the elder of Brooke, esquire.

In December 1658, Richard Cabell, esquire, of Brook(e) Manor, presumably the newly-wed Richard (4), acquired from Sir Courtney Pole, bart., of Shute, for £2,000, the Manors and Lordships of Blackdon Pipard (Blackaton) and Widecombe and all the messuages, tofts, cottages, curtilages, barton buildings, gardens, orchards, etc. within them (DRO 48/14/7/6–8). A schedule of estates excepted from this conveyance is annexed to the release (DRO 48/14/7/7b-c); Middle Bonehill, occupied by Arthur Smerdon holding a 99-year lease, was one of the excluded estates, while what later became Lower Bonehill appears to have been included (because it is not listed in the annex). By May 1659, Richard Cabell was granting leases for various Widecombe messuages (*e.g.*, in Natsworthy, Torr, and Beltorre, DRO 48/14/31/1 & 48/14/52/2a-b). Rennells (1999) noted Richard Cabell leased properties in the heart of Widecombe to John Morrell in 1669; the description of the property in this lease (DRO 48/14/47/2a-b), the initial entry fee (consideration), and annual rent are interesting, *viz*:

> Toft or old walls called the Smitha otherwise the Smitha Mill, with common rights on the commons of the manor of Widicombe; also a little close called Gooseland, on the east side of the grist mills called North Hill Mills, bounded by the sanctuary lands, the highway leading from Widicombe to Bovietracy, and other lands. Also a parcel of land (10 yds.), allotted out by Vincent Andrew the elder of Widicomb, 3 May 1669, and bounded by the highway and toft called the Smitha on the south, the mill leat running to North Hall Mills on the east, and the 6 pits there made in the earth on the north and west.
>
> Consideration: 10s, and agreement by Morrell to rebuild the toft. Rent: 2s 6d.

A toft was the site of a house and its outbuildings, while a close was a small piece of land enclosed by walls, hedges, etc.

Sandles (2007) stated Richard Cabell (Richard 4) died without male issue on 5th July, 1677, (tombstone at Buckfastleigh Church), and that his daughter Elizabeth inherited her father's estates. Richard's Will, made in 1671, was probated in March 1677/8. The Court established administration for Richard's extensive estates in Devon, Wiltshire, Somerset, and Cornwall (including the Dartmoor "Manors of Blackdon Piper and Withecombe", and the tenement of Stone) during the minority of Elizabeth Cabell, his daughter and executrix (DRO 48/14/137/4). However, leases of several Widecombe properties were granted in 1676 by Samuel Cabell of Wivelscombe, Cornwall, esquire (*e.g*, DRO 48/14/31/2a-b). Another 1676 lease effected by Samuel Cabell was of Bunhill Downe to Edward Caunter of Manaton, yeoman (DRO 48/14/51/6a-b). Because of the changes of Lordship of

Widecombe-in-the-Moor described in Chapter 3, it is interesting that this lease to Caunter was passed to George Leyman, yeoman of Widecombe, in 1689 and then, in May 1708, the lease granted by Samuel Cabell was assigned to Samuel Wotton of Englebourne, esquire, after he had become Lord of the Manor (DRO 48/14/51/7).

In the light of the young Elizabeth Cabell's inheritance on her father's death in 1677, the status of Samuel Cabell is not entirely clear; he was probably Richard's (3) brother. Samuel Cabell, esquire, was referred to in 1682 as "lord of premises" of the messuage called "Norwald alias Northhall, and 2 water grist mills belonging" when Ellis Smerdon the elder of Widecombe, yeoman, completed his legal 'surrender' of those properties (DRO 48/14/47/3; *cf.*, Rennells, 1999).

The saga of the transfer of the Manor of Widecombe from Cabell ownership to Wotton family ownership is continued in Chapter 3, but clearly Worthy's (1874, 1875, pp. 61-2) suggestion that, after Queen Elizabeth I's accession to the throne in 1558, the Southcote's Widecombe Estates were "in the family of Wotton", although correct, omitted several very important events. It is now known that Dymond's (1876, p. 26) detailed history is also a little misleading where he wrote:

> The lapse of another century found the manor of Spitchwick, with those of Widecombe and Blagdon Pipard, in the possession of the Wottons of Inglebourne, in the parish of Harberton, where this family had been seated for several generations when the Heralds made their Visitation of Devon in 1620.

Worthy and Dymond's conclusions developed in the 1870s have been generally accepted, but behind the simplicity lies a much more complex story. The three Manors of Widecombe, Blackdon Pipard (Blackaton), and Trusham were caught up in complex trans-actions in the 17th century. Of course, the English Civil Wars also raged and ended before the Wotton's became lords of huge Widecombe-area estates and owners of manors and lands in Holne, Totnes, Staverton, Dartington, and Ashburton Parishes at the beginning of the 18th century.

The reference above to the Visitation is interesting. In the 17th century, the desire for arms by those acquiring gentility rested partly on coat armour being the recognized mark or badge of the gentry. It was the duty of heralds (from the College of Heralds) to make peri-odic "visitations" to check on such coat-armour rights already established, and to assist in determining eligibility of new claimants (*cf.*, Campbell, 1983, p. 35).

Early trackways and field development

In general, the increasing population in Devon had put renewed pressure on land, includ-ing the waste lands, especially that on the higher ground between 600-900 feet (183-275 m); this involved a mixture of re-occupation and expansion into new moorland areas. Hoskins (1954, p. 63) was sure that:

new farms came into being in the 16th and 17th centuries on the upland wastes, and that on the lower ground long-settled farms extended their tillage over the appurtenant moors and commons and brought a larger acreage into permanent use, in place of the extensive and intermittent cultivation of "outfield" ... In the 12th and 13th centuries the creation of new farms had been the characteristic form of colonisation; in the 16th and 17th it was the enlargement of existing farms by taking in of land for tillage and sheep from the surrounding waste.

The term waste was widely used for open moorland and rough uncultivated land, that was sometimes between tilled fields and tended meadows; the waste was often common land used for sheep and cattle pasture. Thus, the term did not have the wholly negative connotation associated with it today. In about 1630, Risdon (1811, p. 6) wrote:

both rocky and heathy, called, by a borrowed name of its barrenness, Dartmoor: richer in its bowels than in the face thereof, yielding tin and turf, which, to save for fuel, you would wonder to see how busy the by dwellers be at some seasons of the year; whose tops and torrs are in the winter often covered with a white cap; but in the summer, the bordering neighbours bring great herds of cattle, and flocks of sheep to pasture there

Both farming and habitation development in Devon have been described in numerous general accounts. As emphasised by Fox (2000), these useful generalisations tend to mask the significant local diversity in arable and stock farming reflecting major variations of soil, elevation, microclimate, etc. across Devon. Specific documentary records are, on the whole, scanty and difficult to fathom but, in addition to occasional buildings (or more commonly ruins and traces of foundations), traces of ancient field units and trackways are reasonably abundant across the county; this is certainly the case around Widecombe-in-the-Moor. Maps of several examples of preserved ancient Devon fields were reproduced by Finberg (1969).

Early tracks serving Widecombe-in-the-Moor included Church Way (known in 1491) heading northwest from Widecombe (around the west end of Hamel Down) and the ancient Lich Way, which crossed the Moor to Lydford. The Mariner's Way passing southwards through Bideford, Throwleigh, Gidleigh, Jurston, Widecombe, Ashburton, and thence on to Dartmouth was apparently a track used by sailors between north and south Devon ports. An east-west trackway from Bovey Tracey through Widecombe to Ponsworthy and Dartmeet, and two tracks from Widecombe southwards down to Ashburton must have been established and used from very early. It has been estimated that well over 10,000 cattle from lowland farms spent each summer on Dartmoor by 1340; large numbers of sheep were also summered on Dartmoor. This considerable transhumance of cattle and sheep to the common lands of Dartmoor for summer grazing between May and October or November contributed significantly to defining routeways from lowland Devon to the Moors. Figure 10, based on Groves (1970, Fig. 23), shows the early roads and tracks over the Moor. Bennett (2007) collated much of the available information about early routes on, or serving, Dartmoor.

Clearly, although access from the outside world was not easy, the agricultural scene in the East Webburn River valley (at the far eastern margin of Widecombe-in-the-Moor Parish) was well developed at an early date, some apparently having been begun in Saxon times (*cf.*, Cocks, 1970, p. 77). Several studies described and illustrated early medieval and earlier strip lynchets and field patterns preserved on the valley sides and hills around Widecombe and adjacent Manaton, especially the much-pictured and studied Challacombe lynchets and Blackaton fields, many of which reflect where pronounced banks (lynchets) were produced by ox-ploughing along the contours (*e.g.*, Hoskins, 1954, Plate 47; Gawne, 1970, pp. 61-3; Cocks, 1970, Fig. 10; Havinden and Wilkinson (1970); Pattison, 1999; Turner, 2005, pp. 40-1). However, the eastern side of the upper East Webburn valley around Bonehill hamlet has received little attention.

Finberg (1969, p. 129, *et seq.*) argued strongly and convincingly that the open-field system, with unfenced strips of land, operated throughout both the steep hillsides and the flatter lowlands of Devon, although until 1950 it was generally agreed this system had never occurred in Devon. He showed that, in a few cases, owned strips were bought and sold until the late 19th century, although many began to disappear before 1300, being incorporated into larger field units. Commonly, only turf balks separated adjacent strips of land which were worked or owned by different people. On steep hillsides (as around Widecombe) ploughing naturally tended to follow the contour, resulting in separately worked strips that broadly followed the contours. In lowland areas, where downhill soil creep was not a major factor, the orientation of the strips of farmed land was more varied, being controlled by miscellaneous local factors. This medieval system of farming in Devon was analogous to the ancient system of semi-communal farming that used to be widespread in Scotland, Wales, and Ireland (*cf.*, Havinden and Wilkinson, 1970). Strip farming was still customary along the northwest coast of Ireland in 1948-50.

Figure 11 shows fields just south of Bloody Foreland, on the northwest Atlantic coast of Donegal, Ireland, where, 60 years ago, the elderly and the very young could always be seen contentedly herding a few cows or sheep on narrow strips of unfenced pasture until dusk. There, on inheritance under the Rundale system, each parcel of land was divided equally between the heirs so the individual subsistence farmers had to work scattered fragments of all types of land. Hill (1868) recorded that in the Gweedore area of northwest Donegal:

> The wretched system of Rundale was in full force, and may be thus described:- In some instances, a tenant owning any part of a townland (no matter how small), had his "proportion" in thirty or forty different places, without fences between them, because the proportions were so numerous. Every tenant considered himself entitled to a portion of each quality of land in his townland; and the man who had some good land at one extremity, was sure to have some bad land at the other, and a bit of middling land in the centre, and bits of other quality in odd corners, each bounded by his neighbours' property, without any fence or ditch between them. Under such circumstances could anyone wonder at the desperation of one poor man, who had his

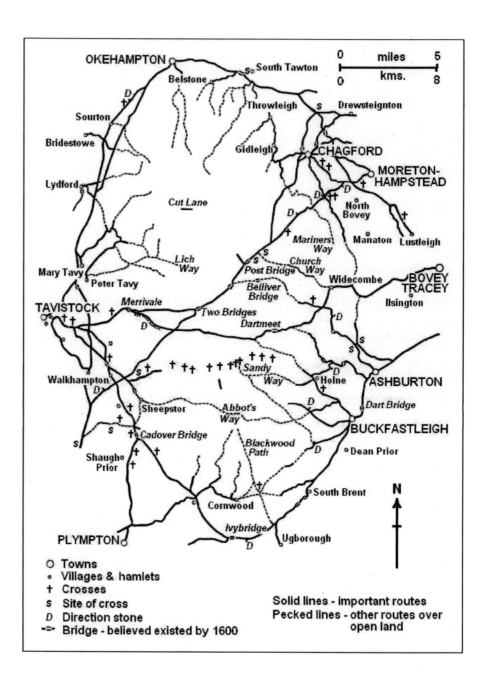

Figure 10. Early roads and tracks across and near Dartmoor before the changes of the last half century (after Groves, 1970, Fig. 23).

52

inheritance in thirty-two different places and abandoned them in despair of ever being able to make them out!

Fights, trespasses, confusion, disputes and assaults, were the natural consequence of this system and these evils were endless, causing great loss of time, and expense to the people in attending petty sessions. The system, too, was a complete bar to any attempt at improvement; on a certain day, all the cattle belonging to the townland were brought from the mountains and allowed to run indiscriminately over the arable land, and any that had not dug their potatoes were much injured; neither could any man venture to grow turnips, clover, or other green crops, for nothing short of a seven feet [2.1 m] wall would keep out the mountain sheep. To add to this, no one would attempt to manure or otherwise improve his proportion, as his neighbour's cattle would have the benefit; and in spring no individual occupier of the division would set or sow, or labour in the fields before a certain day, when the cattle were sent to the hills: and should anyone of them, more industrious or enterprising than another, reclaim a portion of the bog or mountain, it would be taken from him, as soon as he had got one crop off it, and would then be divided among all the tenants of the townland, in proportion to rent paid.

But the system of Rundale was not confined to the land, and the very animals are known to have been quartered by a similar complex tenure.

In the present century, Historic Landscape Characterisation (HLC) studies in Devon have shown that the areas surrounding Bonehill hamlet still retain clear evidence of medieval

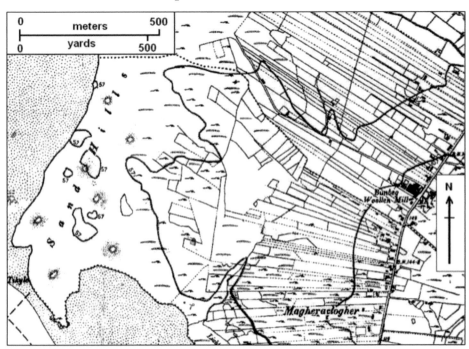

Figure 11. Strip fields near the former Woollen Mill, Middletown, Bunbeg, south of Bloody Foreland, Atlantic coast of Co. Donegal, Ireland; note solid and pecked lines denoting walls and lack of them between strip fields; these fields were still in use until the 1950s. Contours are at 57 and 107 feet above sea level; based on 1906 second edition O.S. Dublin 6 inch/mile (1:10,560) Sheet 32 (SE).

(pre-1600) enclosures based on earlier strip fields (Devon County Council Historic Environment Service, website; Turner, 2005). The resulting maps are freely available on their website. The 3½ year detailed, but broad-brush, study was based on identifying the characteristics of *polygons* (arbitrary map areas normally of more than 1 ha) primarily on the basis of Ordnance Survey Landline mapping, late-19th century first-edition O.S. 25 inch/mile (1:2,500) maps, and 1999-2000 *Getmapping* vertical colour air photographs. Each polygon comprised an arbitrary contiguous polygonal area characterised by similar characteristics. Numerous different landscape-utilisation and field types were defined and mapped. For example, *medieval enclosures based on strip fields* was a type defined by Turner (2005, p. 38) thus:

c. Medieval enclosures based on strip fields

polygons of this type will contain fields with clear evidence for their basis being medieval strip fields. This evidence can take the form of so-called 'aratral curves' (also known as 'reversed s' or 'reversed j' curves) in their boundaries, and/or 'dog-legs'. They are also commonly found in 'regular' field patterns. The difference between these fields and **enclosure (strips)** is that these fields are not necessarily longer than they are wide, and therefore have a significantly different character. The morphology of these fields also differs from **enclosures – post medieval based on medieval strip fields** ... Although both types commonly have sinuous [borders], **Enclosures – medieval based on strip fields** seem to have less regular sides than **enclosures – post-medieval based on strip fields** ... (e.g., boundaries with less regular curves) and closes are generally smaller.

Aratral is not in the Oxford English Dictionary, but must be derived from the obsolete verb aratrate, used in 1656 as meaning "To til or plough, to stir or ear ground". Figure 12 shows the fields around Bonehill hamlet, as recorded on the O.S. 1884 (revised 1904) 6 inch/mile (1:10,560) map sheet *C* (S.W.), the 100-foot topographic contours, and the medieval enclosures based on strip-fields polygons shown on the Devon County Council Historic Environmental Service website map for the post-medieval (c. 1600 – c. 1900) period. While Turner (2005, p. 26) emphasised HLC interpretations provide "... only an initial interpretation based on the limited sources used...", they are an excellent guide for the Bonehill area. It is interesting to compare these structures as seen from the air (Fig. 13) with the interpretive mapping shown in Figure 12.

Across the larger Widecombe area, lynchets or strip fields mainly follow the topographic contours and square-end lynchets are common. If several of the original lynchets were joined together within enclosures, the aratral field boundaries would have been broadly parallel to contours, as is the case around Bonehill. Because the soil in this area abounds in granite boulders and stones, early tillage would have been helped by tediously clearing the ground and piling the granite in banks; so the boundary banks/walls may well date from the initial strip farming; the regular pattern of the fields tends to suggest that an early farmer, having gained ownership or tenancy of several acres, may have built the current boundary pattern over a short period – possibly at about the time the Bonehill granite long-houses were built (the late mid-16th century). A large proportion of these field boundaries is still preserved and used today, commonly now being either Devon banks or granite-boulder walls. However, during the 20th century, mechanisation and changing land use resulted in larger fields being made at the expense of medieval enclosures to the southeast and southwest of Bonehill hamlet (see Figs. 13 and 14 and Historic Landscape Characterisation website's modern map for the c. 1900 to present period).

It must be emphasised that the visual appearance of this landscape changed rapidly during the second half of the 20th century; Figure 14 would have been significantly different if photographed in 1950. Arable land use virtually disappeared around Widecombe-in-the-Moor. Most land is now laid to permanent pasture; fields are only very occasionally ploughed and re-seeded. The changes are obvious by comparing land-use in 1843 (see Fig. 29), when arable dominated with a few pasture fields, and 2001 (Fig. 14) when virtually all fields were permanent-pasture grassland. At the extreme left (north) of Figure 14, three orange-yellow fields are hay fields cut for silage shortly before the photograph was taken in mid-August. So, in this area, ploughing has essentially disappeared, as have haystacks. Although some hay is made into rectangular bales and barn stored, around Widecombe-in-the-Moor in the 21st century, most is baled into large black cylindrical plastic silage sacks, each requiring a tractor to move it; they are conveniently stacked and stored, often in a field corner, until needed to feed stock in winter. A sequence of land-use maps covering the past 75 years would be very informative. The dramatic decline in available manpower on every farm has been accompanied by changed appearance of most hedges, as tractor trimming (often by contractors) has largely replaced traditional manual laying and maintenance.

Mapping the land and the roads

In the 20th and 21st centuries, land ownership has commonly been defined in deeds with the aid of plans and maps; recently, Land Registry Certificates including a detailed map or plan have replaced traditional deeds. However, surveys and descriptions of property until the early 17th century were only verbal, not graphic. For example, a 1608 lease granted by William, Earl of Bath, to Christopher Mudge of Widecombe (DRO 48/14/26/9a-c) referred to

> Piece of waste ground called Lightor Woode (100a.), in the manor of Spichwicke, bounded on the west by the horseway leading from New Bridge to a village called Ayshe, and on the south and east by the river of Darte to Weaborne Foote and from thence to Prowse his bridge up by Copye Lake to Lyttlejohn his Meadowe hedge where heretofore a hedge has been made.

This is much more explicit than customary in most of the lengthy legal indentures of the period, in which there was commonly no mention of area and merely a reference to a property's name, location, or former occupier (*e.g*, tenement at Bonneyhill, or tenement at Bonneyhill formerly in the possession of John Polk). Written descriptions with no graphic

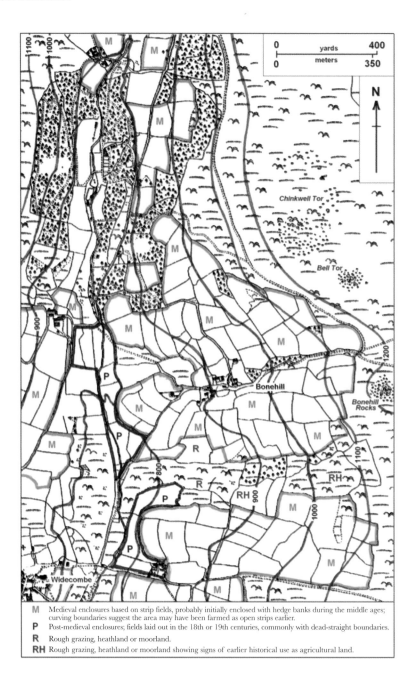

Figure 12. Post-medieval (CE. 1600-1900) historical landscape characteristics astride the East Webburn River valley; the fields around Bonehill hamlet are characterised by medieval enclosures based on earlier strip fields. Topographic contours (in feet) above 1,200 feet (365 meters) are not shown; fletched arrow indicates flow direction of the East Webburn River. Historic landscape characterisation based on Devon County Council Historic Environmental Service website map (see text).

M Medieval enclosures based on strip fields, probably initially enclosed with hedge banks during the middle ages; curving boundaries suggest the area may have been farmed as open strips earlier.

P Post-medieval enclosures; fields laid out in the 18th or 19th centuries, commonly with dead-straight boundaries.

R Rough grazing, heathland or moorland.

RH Rough grazing, heathland or moorland showing signs of earlier historical use as agricultural land.

Figure 13. Satellite image (about noon in May probably 2006) of the Bonehill area in Fig.12, showing the aratal field boundaries of the medieval enclosures.

© Google Earth, 2009.

Figure 14. Evening sunshine over Bonehill hamlet, 16th August, 2001 – view looking just north of east with on the skyline, from south to north, Bonehill Rocks, Bell Tor, and Chinkwell Tor; three aratral fields near left margin were recently cut for silage; larger more-recent straighter field boundaries are seen south of the hamlet; the cluster of oldest Bonehill farmsteads is partially obscured by trees.

definition persisted for decades and, in some places like the Commonwealth of the Bahamas, properties were still defined only textually in legal deeds until late in the 20th century. On the island of Little Elbow Cay, Abaco, land was described as bounded, for example, to the south by the land of William Bethell, to the west by that of Walter Malone, to the …, etc. However, by the late 1980s, the Bahamian government mandated that formal surveyed plats be used for land transactions in Abaco. Occasionally, before maps and plans became common in England, plans were drawn to support legal disputes and have survived. Amazingly, a map of Great Britain (the so-called Gough Map) drawn on animal hides in *ca*. 1360 shows "dertesmour" (Dartmoor) inland from "dertemouth" (Dartmouth) and "Plymouth"; "aschperton" (Ashburton) is also named. Unfortunately, Dartmoor was illustrated as a circle (with a river flowing south to the sea) and this circle was reproduced as a lake on famous 16th century maps printed by Münster in Switzerland and Lilly in Italy (Millea, 2007).

The earliest preserved maps specifically of Dartmoor are diagrammatic. Ravenhill and Rowe (2000, p. 5; 2002, pp. 159-160, entry 4/3/1) mentioned a late-15th or early-16th century map now in the Devon Record Office (DRO, 3950Z/Z1). It depicts Dartmoor as a circle with streams (in blue) flowing out from it; bridges are in brown, areas outside the Moor are coloured green, gates are shown marking the commoners' rights of way to the Moor, and numerous names and Dartmoor boundary marks are shown within scrolls. Roads are depicted as "… reddish-brown between red lines for principal routes; single red and reddish-brown for less-important roads; moorland tracks white between black lines" (Ravenhill and Rowe, 2002, p.160). Worth (1967, p. 332) described a slightly later map, comprising four concentric circles, that is in a document prepared in 1542 for a Commission attempting to document lands thought to belong to the Prince of Wales within the Forest of Dartmoor; it is entitled *Informacions for my lorde prynce to the kynges most Honorable Counsell concernyng my said Lrde prynces Forest of Dartmoor in the Countye of Devonshire &c in the mores and wastes of the same belongyn* (Ravenhill and Rowe, 2000, p. 5; 2002, p. 160, entry 4/3/2) and is preserved in the Public Record Office (PRO S.C. 12/2/39). Worth considered this a very good picture of Devon, as viewed from the perspective of "the true Dartmoor man"; he wrote of the Forest at the centre

> with its ancient tenements and their owners and occupiers; then a belt of common land, in many parishes [including Widecombe], but unified by common rights exercised over all but minor areas; ... [then a belt] of parishes in vills in venville, where lived the venville tenants whose rights were second only to those of the ancient tenements... [Outside lay the rest of the county,] the land of the 'strange men' and 'foreigners or wreytors (writers)', who none the less had their own rights on the Commons of Devon and in the Forest excepting the inhabitants of Totnes and Barnstaple.

An account of the bounds of Dartmoor affecting Buckfast Abbey shortly after 1553 was illustrated with a map of Dartmoor which merely comprised three concentric circles (see Ravenhill and Rowe, 2000, p. 4, Map 1; 2002, pp. 160-1, entry 4/3/3). The Forest of Dartmoor is in the innermost circle; the middle ring represents moors between the Forest and the fields of the hillside; the outer ring is the private tilled and inhabited areas, with four gates (south, east, north, and west) into the middle zone.

Glebe terriers (surveys) were ordered to be made in English dioceses in the 16th century to combat church property passing into lay ownership after the Reformation. The earliest extant glebe terriers in Exeter Diocese are all written surveys of the lands, with the sole exception of that for 77.5 acres (31.36 ha) at Shirwell, a north Devon parish, where the parish clerk in 1601 provided a detailed map with roads and tracks; this map was reproduced by Ravenhill and Rowe (2000, Map 11, pp. 24-5; see also 2002, p. 311, entry 18/14/1).

A copy of a Dartmoor map drawn as a circle was used in a legal dispute as recently as 1786; it had probably been drawn to illustrate pasture and venville rights of the manorial lords of

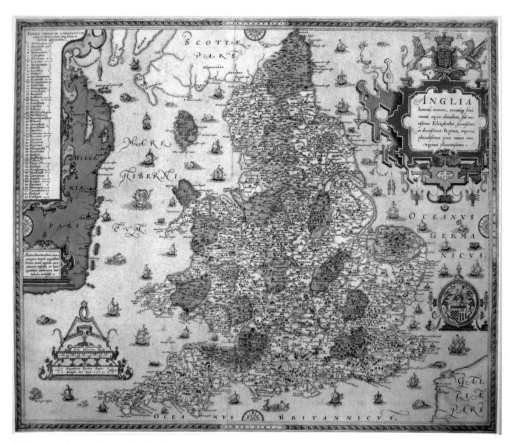

Figure 15. Anglia, Christopher Saxton's 1579 printed map of England and Wales. (From a private collection; reproduced with permission.)

Ugborough at the end of the 15th century (Harvey, 1980, p. 97); Ravenhill and Rowe's (2000, Map 1a, p. 4) facsimile shows details of several rivers like the Dart and Tavy (Ravenhill and Rowe, 2002, p. 162 entry 4/3/7).

Significant rural property, developed in the mid-16th century, is confirmed by surviving contemporary tax assessments and by the quality of farmhouses still remaining today, the majority of which were rebuilt or substantially modernised between 1560 and 1640. Before this building was undertaken, there must have been a generation or two of high prosperity and considerable savings, even if the actual building was financed by lords of manors (often with wealth accrued from commerce), and/or partially supported by mortgages. In Bonehill hamlet, and Widecombe-in-the-Moor generally, evidence of such fine farmhouses and out-buildings still abounds. Indeed, as detailed in Chapters 3 and 4, the current Lower Bonehill farmhouse was built in the late mid-16th century and Middle Bonehill farmhouse a little later.

Figure 16. *Devoniae Comitat, rerumquae...*, The County of Devon; Christopher Saxton's 1579 printed map. Size of original map 40.0 x 44.5 cm (15.75 x 17.52 in). (From a private collection; reproduced with permission.)

Towards the end of the 16th century, accurate land surveying by triangulation became possible, as evidenced by Christopher Saxton's elegant and beautiful map *Anglia*, which showed every county of England and Wales (Fig. 15) and reflected his own detailed surveying. This map was incorporated in a fine Atlas (Saxton, 1579) that can rarely be seen today, although readily available in facsimile (Ravenhill, 1992). The Atlas included the first printed map of the County of Devon, *Devoniae Comitat, rerumquae ....* (Fig. 16); a proof copy was printed in 1575. This map measures 40.0 x 44.5 cm (15.75 x 17.52 in) and is surprisingly accurate; Webbicombe (Widecombe-in-the-Moor) and Buckland with their churches are shown clearly, as is the (unnamed) Dartmeet Bridge, although there is no indication of any roads or of the administrative hundreds.

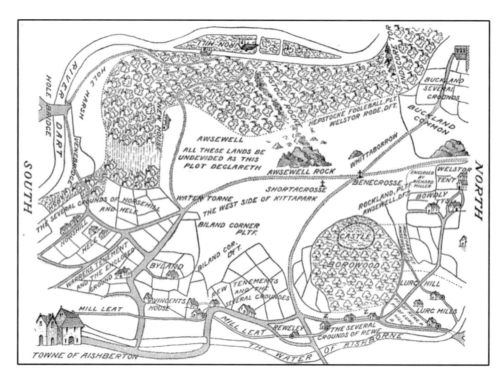

Figure 17. Part of the Manor of Ashburton as redrawn by Amery (1925, p. 94) from the original untitled coloured map in the Public Records Office, originally prepared in 1605 as evidence for a legal dispute; west was at the top of the original map, which measured 44.5 x 59.4 cm (17.5 x 23.4 in).

A beautiful map (*ca.* 44.5 x 59.4 cm; 17.5 x 23.4 in) drawn in about 1604-5 of land between the Rivers Dart and Ashburn (Yeo), from Ashburton in the southwest to Buckland in the northeast, is preserved in the Public Record Office. The scale is roughly 10 inches to a mile (*ca.* 1:634,000) although the map is considerably compressed from east to west; as was not unusual at the time, the map was drawn with north to the right. A small redrawn uncoloured version (Fig. 17; Amery, 1925, p. 94) and a coloured facsimile (Ravenhill and Rowe, 2000, Map 12, p 26; see also 2002, p. 55, entry 1/8/1) are readily accessible. The original map was appended to written depositions for a legal dispute over property boundaries affecting copyholders of Aishberton Manor. It showed the roads quite accurately (represented by parallel lines and coloured pale brown) radiating north-eastwards from Ashburton; they match the main roads on 19th century Ordnance Survey maps, although 20th-century roads have replaced those between Aishberton and Hole Bridge (Ashburton and Holne Bridge) across the River Dart. The main road north from the Towne of Aishberton was shown swinging across The Water of Aishborne (Ashburn River, now the River Yeo) and the Mill Leat, before climbing to Benecrosse (now Auswell Cross) and Buckland; a less-well defined branch road was shown at Benecrosse (as now) to Welstor (on the map's north margin) - which approximates the course of the present road to Cold East Cross and thence to Widecombe-in-the-Moor. So, the route of the current public road from Ashburton to Widecombe was well established by 1600, although, of course, its condition was probably very poor, even for packhorses. For perspective, note that a regular carrier service out of Exeter developed only by the 17th century; the first passenger coach service into Devon started on three days a week in 1658, with the London to Exeter route *via* Salisbury, Dorchester, and Axminster taking four days and costing £2 (Bennett, 2007, p. 84; Hoskins, 1954, p. 150).

In the centuries after the Norman Conquest (see Chapter 2), the concept and practice of homage controlled the structure of English society, but this had gradually evolved until, in the Tudor period, "... the influence of the patron who could unlock the royal bounty and put pressure on his friends, relations, and political acquaintances" was the dominating principle at every level of society (Smith, 2006, pp. 131-48). It was a time when the universe was believed to be filled with purpose that was dominated by the opposing forces of right and wrong. When problems arose, a scapegoat was necessary, rather than finding a moral or other failing in one's self – it was (Smith 2006, p. 131 and 139)

> far easier and infinitely more satisfying to look for the cause of life's catastrophes and personal failures in witchcraft, the evil eye, the interference of demons, and above all in the conspiracy of an enemy. ... [So the] cure for social evil was almost invariably the same – root out and destroy the wrongdoer; rarely did it encompass the mitigation or reform of the forces that stood behind social malfunction and tension.

The practical consequences and some perspective about local life in this era were provided by Hoskins (1954, pp. 251-3). He recalled that 74 people were hanged in Devon in 1598, more than half of these having been condemned at Quarter Sessions, and that capital crimes included horse-stealing, cutting a purse, picking pockets, house breaking, receiving stolen goods, and sheep stealing; at Easter that year, it was ordered that every woman who had a bastard child be whipped. Puritan influences were strong in England. In 1599, the Puritan justices in Devon ordered that parish games, church ales, and revels should be utterly suppressed because they were occasions for behaviour "which with modestie cannot be expressed", although such revels and parish feasts were officially restored after 1660. Queen Elizabeth I died in 1603, the gunpowder plot occurred in 1605, and the Pilgrim Fathers inaugurated religious migration to New England in 1620. Between 1625 (the year of James I's death) and 1626, many parts of Devon were affected badly from the dreaded plague, which returned at numerous times over the next four decades; in 1626, Ashburton suffered 464 deaths and up to 2,300 died in Exeter. Andriette (1971, p. 25) recorded, on the basis of various contemporary reports, that:

> Weekly rates were levied and collected from adjacent hundreds in order to provide support for the growing number of people forcibly shut up within the infected districts. During the 1625-6 period the heavy burden of these rates, and the widespread nature of the disease, was reflected

in the increased number of communities calling upon their neighbours for support. From the general rates ... Totnes, Ashburton, Buckland, and North Bovey [received] £150 a week between them,

Despite the overall trends through the 17th century, the concept of homage persisted into the 18th century within rural Manors, as shown by the Court Rolls of the Manor of Widecombe-in-the-Moor (see Figure 22).

In this period, there was considerable local specialisation in the Devon woollen industry and, by the end of the 17th century, Ashburton had become one of the county's principal spinning districts (Hoskins, 1954, p. 128).

Writing in 1638, Risdon (1811, p. 4) had noted in his survey of Devon that:

This country, as it is spacious, so it is populous, and very laborious, rough, and unpleasant to strangers travelling those ways, which are cumbersome and uneven, amongst rocks and stones, painful for man and horse; as they can best witness who have made trial thereof. For be they never so well mounted upon horses out of other countries, when they have travelled one journey in these parts, they can, in respect of ease of travel, forbear a second. And therefore so much the less passable for the enemy, with his troops of war

Chapple's (1785, pp. 13-5) preferred rendition of Risdon's 1638 manuscript* was:

As this Country is spacious, so it is populous; but the Roads in the hilly Lands are very laborious and fatiguing, rough and unpleasant to Strangers unaccustomed to travel in such Ways; being cumbersome and uneven, in some Parts deep and miry, in others rocky and stony, painful for Men and Horse; as was sufficiently experienced by those of the more Eastern and less hilly Counties, who had Occasion to travel our Roads before any Turnpikes were erected: For were they ever so well mounted upon Horses out of their own Country, when they had travelled one Journey is these Parts, they could gladly have forborne the Fatigue of a second. This Roughness of our Roads was formerly deem'd an Advantage to this County, it being so much the less passable for the Troops and Carriages of an Enemy in Time of War:

Cromwell is reputed to have claimed Devon was the best-farmed county in England, but the 17th century was a time of great upheaval, extraordinary development, and change in almost every sphere of endeavour. In all probability, Devon as a whole had become overpopulated. The Civil War began in 1642 and Hoskins (1954, p. 86), writing about Devon in general, noted:

the Interregnum impoverished the royalist gentry very considerably, but did not break them. The county was much fought over, country houses sacked, farms devastated and robbed, and in addition the royalist landlords were heavily fined for their "delinquency" according to their support for the King's cause.

*Risdon is difficult to cite: he completed his manuscript in 1630 but continued with a few updates until 1638, about two years before he died; he was born 1581. About 70 years later, a copy of the manuscript was used by Edmund Curll to print corrupted versions in 1714 and 1725. William Chapple obtained a copy of the original Risdon manuscript and began, in 1772, to edit and publish the whole but, by the time of his death in 1781, only the first pages had been tackled; what he had completed was published in 1785 and a facsimile appeared in 1970. An apparently genuine version of Risdon's original manuscript was published in Plymouth in 1811, as cited above.

Sir Humphrey Tracy of Bovey Tracey had to pay one of the heaviest fines in Devon. Numerous books deal with the Civil War and its consequences in Exeter, Plymouth, and indeed all the land around the Moor, but none seems to refer to whether rural life on Dartmoor itself was impacted significantly by the turmoil. It is tempting to suppose Civil War pressures rumbled around the flanks of the Moor without causing too many ripples amongst actual occupants of the higher settlements. While throughout the southwest in general, the peers and greater gentry stood on the King's side and the lesser gentry and townsfolk for Parliament, Devon as a whole seems to have been more parliamentarian than royalist, although many tenants tended to side with their landlords and may have found it difficult to do otherwise. The manorial lords of Widecombe-in-the-Moor, Spitchwick, and Blackaton were certainly royalists, although their living outside the Moor probably lessened their direct interaction with the Widecombe-area yeomen and the rest of the farming community. However, there were many folk on each side, and the issues even divided some notable families (*cf.*, Hoskins, 1954, p. 195). Certainly the fines imposed by Parliamentarians, and sometimes the subsequent restoration of fines, significantly impacted ownership of Widecombe's manors and estates, and may have indirectly affected life of the community (see Chapter 3). Hoskins (1954, pp. 65-6) considered that, by the middle of the 17th century:

> there were too many people looking for land and too many looking for work in Devon; the results were low wages, unemployment and under-employment, poverty, bad housing, insecurity, and emigration to New England. But at the other extreme of the social scale, fortunes were being made, and successful merchants were buying country estates ... and founding new county families.

Irrespective of the Civil Wars, the abundance of fine farmhouses surviving in and around Widecombe-in-the-Moor from this period shows that many of the trends affecting the rest of Devon are, indeed, also reflected high on the Moor.

All moorland routes must have continued to be extremely challenging, as were even the trunk routes in lowland Devon. The first printed maps to show roads in Devon were strip maps in Ogilby's (1675) Britannia, ... Although somewhat primitive by current standards, Ogilby's Plate 27 included the Exeter to Plymouth road, with three side roads between Bickington and Ashburton labelled "to y Moor" -- these match the current roads across Ashburton Down to Cold East Cross; Plate 69, the Exeter to Truro road *via* Chagford across Dartmoor to Tavistock, showed turn offs to "Withecomb" at the extant road south of Merripit Hill - 6 miles (9.6 km) west of Chagford - and also immediately east of the "Poft bridg", the Postbridge clapper bridge.

The first printed map of the County of Devon to show roads was tiny, being the IX of Diamonds (Fig. 18) in Morden's (1676) decks of playing cards; Ogilby's (1675) two roads (Exeter to Plymouth and Exeter to Tavistock) were depicted. Five years later, Blome's (1681)

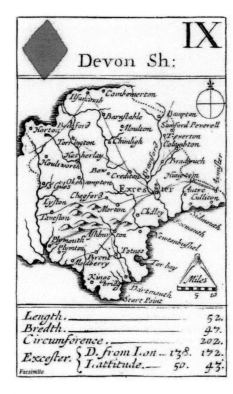

Figure 18. IX of Diamonds from deck of playing cards printed by Robert Morden in 1676; each card portrayed a different county. Original card was 90 x 55 mm; the map panel for Devon being 5.8 x 5.5 cm.(2.28 x 2.17 in). From facsimile published by Harry Margary, 1972).

Atlas, *Speed's Maps Epitomiz'd*, included *A Mapp of Devon Shire* with numerous roads; for example, those from Chagford to Ashburton and from Chagford to Dean Prior, which were shown passing equal distances east and west of "Withycombe".

The first printed map of the county with a road passing through Widecombe appeared in John Overton's (1685) *Atlas III* published in London (see Fig. 19). This 38 x 49 cm map, *Devoniae Descriptio*, is a close copy of a Dutch map of 1652 by Jan Jansson, but with roads added somewhat diagrammatically; Jansson's name was retained on the map. A road branching off the Chudleigh to Ashburton road at Bovey Tracey passes WSW through Widecombe, over Ponsworthy Bridge (a stone in which is dated 1666), across the Dartmeet clapper bridge, and then across the moors to Tavistock. This route is closely followed by present-day roads (*cf*, Groves, 1970; see Fig. 10). Philip Lea (1694) issued *The Shires of England and Wales* with a new engraving titled *DEVON=SHIRE Described by C. Saxton Corrected, Amended and many Additions by P. Lea.* This was copied from Christopher Saxton's 1575 county map but was newly engraved by Francis Lamb. Numerous roads were added; the Bovey Tracey - Widecombe - Tavistock road is intersected by the Buckland - Widecombe - Chagford and the Ashburton - Moretonhampstead roads (Fig. 20). Considering the nature of the roads at that time, these 17th century maps are quite remarkable.

A measure of the quality of trunk roads in Devon comes from Celia Fiennes' report after the Civil War in the summer of 1698. This Cromwellian colonel's daughter and ardent Non-Conformist, travelled on horseback westwards along the main road from Exeter through Chudleigh and Ashburton to Plymouth. Her journal recorded (Morris, 1982, p. 200):

> From Chedly [Chudleigh] to Ashburton a poor little town, bad was the best Inn; its a Market town and here are a great many Descenters and those of the most considerable persons in the town, there was a Presbiterian an Anabaptist and Quakers meeting. Thence I went for Plymouth and here the roades contracts and the lanes are exceeding narrow and so cover'd up you can see little about, an army might be marching undiscover'd by any body ... the wayes now became so difficult that one could scarcely pass by each other, even the single horses, and so dirty in many

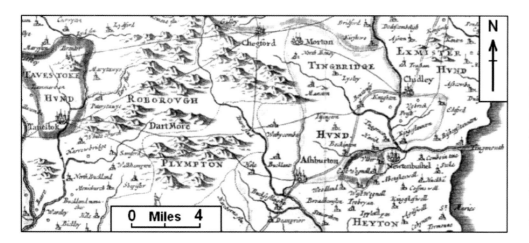

Figure 19. Small part of the first printed map to show a road through Widecombe-in-the-Moor, from Overton's *Devoniae Descriptio*, first printed in *Overton Atlas III*, London, 1685 – the road from Chudleigh to Tavistock crosses East Dart River at Dartmeet (just west of Widecombe). From Batten and Bennett's (1996, p. 39) illustration of the 1690 edition *Overton Atlas IV*.

places and just a track for one horses feete, and the banks on either side so neer, and were they not well secured and mended with stones struck close like a drye wall every where when they discover the bancks to breake and molder down which else would be in danger of swallowing up the way quite, ...

About 4 or 5 mile [6.4 or 8.0 km] from Ashburton I came to a little place called Dean and at the end of it ascended a very steep hill, all rock almost and so it was like so many steps up; this is called Dean Clapperhill, it was an untoward place but not soe formidable to me as the people of the place where I lay described it, haveing gone much worse hills in the North [of England]; all along on the road where the lanes are a little broader you ride by rowes of trees on each side set and kept exactly even and cut, the tops being for shade and beauty, and they in exact forme, as if a grove to some house; ... all their carriages are here on the backs of horses with sort of hookes like yoakes stands upon each side of a good height, which are the receptacles of their goods, either wood furse or lime or coal or corn or hay or straw, or what else they convey from place to place; and I cannot see how two such horses can pass each other or indeed in some places how any horse can pass by each other, and yet these are the roads that are all here abouts; some little corners may jutt out that one may get out of the way of each other, but this but seldom.

Fiennes also wrote (Morris, 1982, p. 196):

you meete all sorts of country women wrapp'd up in the manteles called West Country rockets [rochets], a large mantle doubled together of a sort of serge, some are linsywolsey, and a deep fringe or fag at the lower end; these hang down some to their feete some only just below the wast, in the summer they are all in white garments of this sort, in the winter they are in red ones; I call them garments because they never go out without them and this is the universal fashion in Sommerset and Devonshire and Cornwall.

Note that Miss Fiennes wrote only about the main road south of the Moor. As late as 1786, William Simpson (1786), a Duchy of Cornwall surveyor, wrote (as quoted by Groves, 1970, p. 194) that:

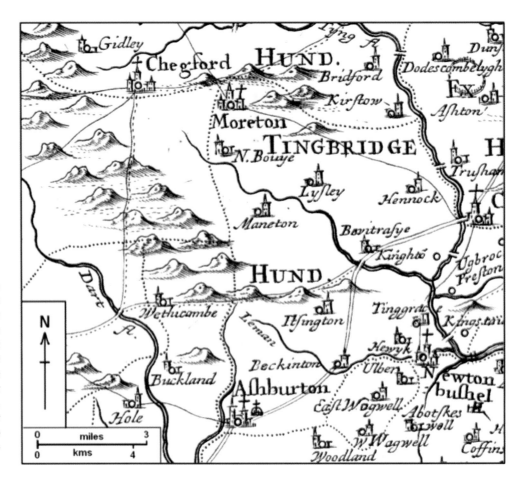

Figure 20. Roads around Wethicombe (Widecombe-in-the-Moor), shown on Philip Lea's newly engraved map *DEVON=SHIRE* of 1694 which was printed at the scale of 283,879:1 (about 3.85 miles/inch). Main roads are shown by double lines (one of the lines pecked on lesser roads); minor roads were shown by single solid lines. The administrative Hundreds and their boundaries (dotted lines) are also represented. (From a private collection; reproduced with permission.)

within the last twenty years there were only three or four very blind roads across the whole [of Dartmoor], insomuch that going over the moor in winter was always considered not only as an arduous but really dangerous undertaking; and the many lives lost in such attempts is too notorious to be doubted.

Despite what these travellers thought, Widecombe had wool-tucking mills in the 17th century and a thriving cloth industry well into the 18th century (Booker, 1970, p. 121); the products were despatched by packhorse to Ashburton and other places for marketing. By the early 19th century, wagons from a large woollen mill at Chagford used the road across the Moor just south of Widecombe-in-the-Moor, going by New House tavern (long since disappeared) and Cold East Cross, and thence to Ashburton (*cf.*, Groves, 1970, p. 191).

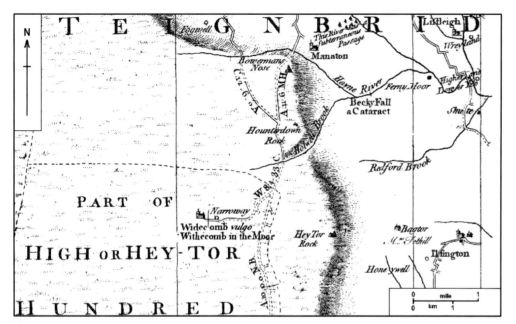

Figure 21. The Widecombe area from Donn's (1765) 1″/mile (1:63,360) printed map of Devon; note the boundary between Hey-tor and Teignbridge Hundreds just north and east of Widecombe church. Donn showed distances along main roads – for example, Widecombe to Chagford is 8 miles 4 furlongs & 33 poles and Ashburton to North Bovey is exactly 10 miles *via* the road passing east of Widecombe (1 mile or 1.609 km is 8 furlongs; a furlong is 40 poles). From facsimile printed by Devon and Cornwall Record Society and the University of Exeter, 1965, Sheet 6b.

Hemery (1983, p. 654) drew attention to Thornhill Lane having been in regular use as a horse-and-wagon road between Natsworthy and Ashburton; today, this bouldery track climbs from Natsworthy to the west of Honeybag Tor, crosses Bonehill Lane (just above Bonehill Gate) and can be traced to the main road at the top of Widecombe Hill.

The quality of Overton's (1685) and Lea's (1694) maps is remarkably good when compared with Benjamin Donn's (1765) prize-winning and much applauded 1 inch to the mile [1:63,360] Devon map produced from his actual surveying. Donn showed clearly the north-south road from Chagford to Ashburton, which became so extensively used by wagons in the early nineteenth century and lies, as today, mid-way between "Hey Tor Rock" and Widecombe Church. However, the only road Donn showed serving Widecombe itself forked off south of Holwell Brook (just within the Parish boundary), skirted east of Bonehill Rocks, to descend a partially walled road just east and south of "Narroway" and then terminate at the church (Fig. 21). The farm track along the eastern boundary of Northway Farm (leading from Widecombe Hill to the 21st century Upper Northway Farmhouse) appears to use part of that old road. Thornhill Lane track was not shown. So, Donn's map seems deficient around "Widecomb *vulgo* Withecomb in the Moor" if, indeed, there was any other route to the village worthy of being called a road in 1765.

3

LORDSHIP AND ESTATE OWNERSHIP
ABOUT WIDECOMBE AROUND 1700

It seems highly probable that John Southcote of Indio, Bovey Tracey, owned the land about Bonehill at the end of the 16th century, and that he commissioned the building of the principal farmhouse at Lower Bonehill in 1550, or a little thereafter, and then Middle Bonehill somewhat later. It is unknown who initially lived in these farmhouses and worked the farm/s. Clearly, however, the Bonehill farmsteads were active long before most of the Widecombe property was acquired by Sir Courtney Pole and then purchased by Richard Cabell (4) in 1658, after the restoration of at least some of his Civil War fines. The appendix to an Indenture dated 1658 (DRO 48/14/7/7c) recorded that Arthur Smerdon possessed an on-going 99-year lease to Bonehill (apparently Middle Bonehill), which might suggest that, at one time, the Smerdon family held lease/s from the Southcote family.

As noted in Chapter 2, the Civil Wars had caused much turmoil in Devon and, as Bagehot (2008, p. 40) wrote, the period of strife throughout England (and beyond) had been very

> messy, and not just in terms of gore. It lacks heroes as "1066 and All That", a comic guide to English history summarises, the Roundheads were "right but repulsive". They banned Christmas and succumbed to militarism and murder. The revolution was halting, sometimes inadvertent and superficially undone by the Restoration. Moreover, it was a parliamentary rather than popular revolt, and so transformed ordinary lives less than some other upheavals: it did not bequeath a general sense of civic pride and participation, as did the American and French revolutions that it helped to inspire.

Charles II had been restored to the monarchy in 1660, the Great Fire of London followed in 1666, and 1685 saw the death of Charles II. Issues surrounding the Lordship of the Manor of Widecombe-in-the-Moor and the adjacent manors and properties were left in Chapter 2 at around 1677 (Elizabeth's inheritance, as a minor, of Richard Cabell's (4) estates) and 1682, when Samuel Cabell – probably Richard Cabell's (3) brother - was granting leases for properties in and around Widecombe.

The Lordships of the Manors of Widecombe, Blagdon-Pipard (Blackaton), and Spitchwick in the two decades either side of 1700 were very significant in Bonehill's evolution. This was because, apart from a few relatively small estates or farmsteads whose owners possessed the freehold, all the lands and estates were owned by the Lord of each Manor. These Lords were effectively absentee, living beyond the fringes of Dartmoor or, in some cases, outside the county. Most of the manorial lands were either leased by indenture to tenants for a few years or, very commonly, farmsteads were leased for 99-years or three lives (explained below). Thus, freehold, three-lives leases, and short-term leases were all relevant to Bonehill hamlet around 1700.

Cabell, D'Oyly, to Wotton

Sometime after 1683, Samuel Cabell moved from Buckfastleigh to South Petherton, which is about 5 miles (8 km) north of Crewkerne, Somerset. On 25th March, 1685, he granted a three-lives lease for Bonneyhill (one part of what later became Lower Bonehill) to yeoman John Polk of Widecombe (DRO 48/14/43/1). Four years later (May 1689), Samuel leased another messuage and tenement which was also merely called Bonneyhill (the second part of the eventual Lower Bonehill – apparently, the present Lower Bonehill farmhouse) to William Cauntor, yeoman of Widecombe (DRO 48/14/43/2). This 1689 traditional three-lives lease, for a consideration of £175, was on the life of William Cauntor, his son William Cauntor, and Jane Brooking (daughter of Phillipp Brooking of Widecombe, blacksmith).

Another 1689 lease granted by Samuel Cabell was for the "Mansion house or capital messuage called Northhall alias Norrald" and two grist mills for a consideration of £200 and two broad pieces of gold; the annual rent was 30s. (DRO 48/14/47/4). Smitha cottage and Gooseland by Northhall were also leased in 1694 to Ellize Andrew, yeoman (DRO 48/14/75/5).

In 1693 (see Table 2 for chronology), some 16 years after the young Elizabeth Cabell inherited Richard (4) Cabell's estates in 1677, she married Cholmeley D'Oyly, heir and oldest child of Sir John D'Oyly of Chiselhampton, a village just southeast of Oxford (Djabri, 1991). There was extremely varied spelling of D'Oyly in legal documents, sometimes even in the same document.

By a deed dated 1694, Samuel Cabell of South Petherton, esquire, completed his elaborate marriage settlement of lands worth £500 on his wife Elizabeth for her lifetime; this deed made clear he had no children by his wife (SAR: DD\PE/18: Release of lands in Somerset, Wiltshire, Devon and Cornwall, 22 January, 1694/5). This completion included the "manors of Blackdon Piper and Withycombe in Devon, and other lands in the parish of Widecombe in the Moor (called Stone Rowbrookes, Torr and Hannaford)". The *term* of this deed was Samuel's life, and it was also a release of all of his assets, after his and Elizabeth's deaths, to his sons born of Elizabeth (there were none) and then to his two widowed sisters Julian Roope of Little Dartmouth and Susannah Wotton of Englebourne, Devon, and their heirs; this implies Samuel's sister, Susannah Cabell, had become the widow, Mrs. Susannah Wotton.

Intriguingly, a Latin document of 1700 concerns a 'fine' involving John D'Oyly, esquire, plaintiff, and Samuel Wotton, esquire, deforciant, and huge estates all over Devon and Cornwall, including the Manor of Englebourne and some Widecombe properties, and the consideration of £1,660 (DRO 48/14/137/6a-b); a deforciant is a person who keeps the rightful owner of an estate out of possession. Undoubtedly, an interesting story behind this

Table 2
Widecombe and Bonehill ownership and occupation history – 1680-1750

1683: Samuel Cabell moved from Buckfastleigh to South Petherton, Somerset, sometime after 1683.

1685: John Polk granted three-lives lease of Bonneyhill (? southern part of Lower Bonehill) by Samuel Cabell.

1689: William Cauntor granted three-lives lease of Bonneyhill, lately occupied by John Smerdon, by Samuel Cabell; this appears to be the current Lower Bonehill farmhouse.

1693: Elizabeth Cabell (the daughter) married Cholmeley D'Oyly of Oxford (who died in 1700).

1694: Samuel Cabell completed his marriage settlement, adding Manors of Widecombe and Blackdon Piper and numerous Widecombe estates to the settlement (all presumably his to settle - ?).

----: A marriage settlement apparently made under which Elizabeth D'Oyly (neé Cabell) to pay Sir John D'Oyly (Cholmeley's father) £10,000.

1699: Cholmeley and Elizabeth D'Oyly sold Widecombe and Blackdon Pipard estates – John and Susanna D'Oyly new owners.

1700: John D'Oyly's (Cholmeley's brother) settlement against Samuel Wotton over Englebourne Manor and other widespread properties.

1700: Cholmeley D'Oyly died, childless, and Elizabeth discovered Cholmeley had secretly married another before marrying her; she attempts to negate the £10,000 marriage-settlement payment due to Sir John D'Oyly – Chancery Court proceedings followed.

1701: Elizabeth D'Oyly (widow) married Richard Fownes and subsequently lost her Chancery case (and the appeal); is required to pay the £10,000 to Sir John D'Oyly, plus massive legal fees.

1701: Samuel Cabell died (Cabells ceased to be Lords of Widecombe Manor); Samuel Wotton and Elizabeth Fownes were serving as Executors of Samuel Cabell's Will.

1701 & 1703: Widecombe Court Rolls show Court headed by Elizabeth Cabell (the widow of Cholmeley D'Oyly)..

1703-5: Doyly (D'Oyly) apparent ownership of Widecombe estates. (John Doyly was Cholmeley Doyly's heir).

1705: Samuel Wotton acquired (£2,250) freehold to Manor of Widecombe and other local tenements (including Lower Bonehill, then called Bonneyhill) from John and Susanna D'Oyly who were apparently owners since 1699.

1707: Samuel Wotton acquired (£800) freehold to Manor of Blagdon Pipard, etc.

1707: Court Rolls show Samuel Wotton Lord of Widecombe-in-the-Moor.

1711: John Hannaford granted three-lives lease of the part of Bonneyhill (Lower Bonehill) previously leased to John Polk (died 1701).

1714: Samuel Wotton acquired Manor of Spitchwick.

1715: Robert Hannaford granted three-lives lease of part of Bonneyhill (main Lower Bonehill farmhouse) previously occupied by Rᵈ Tremills (apparently after William Cauntor's occupation).

1735: Following Samuel Wotton's death, son William inherited Widecombe Lordship and estates but died 1742; his brother Rev. John Wotton inherited Lordship in 1743.

1745: Final deed establishing Wotton (not D'Oyly) title to Widecombe estates.

1746 (5 Nov.): Rev. John Wotton died; under his Will a 99-year trust created to raise £2,000 for his only child (infant Anna Maria) – the three trustees were Sir Thomas D'Oyly, John Shapleigh, Rev. Henry Holdsworth.

1747-52: Richard Wotton (John's younger brother) was Lord of Widecombe Manor until his death.

1769: John Dunning, MP bought the Widecombe, Spitchwick, etc. properties for the residual remaining term under the Wotton trust.

settlement lies buried in history. The 19th century writers (Worthy, 1874, 1875; Dymond 1876) asserted that the Wotton family bought the Manor of Englebourne from the Crown in 1546 and the basis for D'Oyly's intervention in 1700 is currently unexplained, although it may not be unrelated to the saga surrounding Cholmeley D'Oyly's role in the history of Widecombe property. John and Cholmeley D'Oyly were brothers; there seem to have been close family links between some members of the Wotton and D'Oyly families.

After Cholmeley's death in Buckfastleigh in 1700, his widow, Elizabeth D'Oyly (neé Cabell), learned he had previously secretly married the daughter of a poor clergyman (Djabri, 1991, p. 5), so she

> immediately tried to overturn her marriage settlement, under which she had to pay £10,000 to Sir John, but the earlier marriage was declared invalid, and she had to pay not only the debt but also the heavy costs of the chancery case and appeal.

It appears Cholmeley and Elizabeth D'Oyly had sold the Widecombe and Blackdon Pipard estates (which Elizabeth had inherited from her father) in June 1699 and the properties had become owned by John D'Oyly and his wife Susanna (see Indenture dated November 1705 - DRO 48/14/8/1b). Before the end of Elizabeth's Chancery case attempting to escape the £10,000 payment to Sir John, she married Richard Fownes of South Petherton, esquire; Richard and Elizabeth's 1701 marriage settlement survives in the Somerset Archives (SAR DD/PE).

Samuel Cabell ceased to be cited as Lord of the Manor of Widecombe-in-the-Moor after 1700. Elizabeth Cabell appears at the head of Widecombe Court Rolls for 1701 (Fig. 22) and 1703 (DRO 48/14/1/15). Numerous familiar names, like John Smerdon, are referred to in these Rolls; the death of John Polk, conventionary tenant of the Manor for a tenement at "Bonhill", was noted in 1701. In October 1701, Elizabeth Cabell of Brooke leased the cottage and milling house, lately in possession of Margaret Milward, to blacksmith Phillipp Brooking for the consideration of £5 and yearly rent of 1s. (DRO 48/14/54/8a,b). By 1703, Samuel Wotton of Englebourne, esquire, and Elizabeth Fownes (the recently re-married daughter of Richard (4) Cabell) were serving as executors of the late Samuel Cabell's Will (DRO 48/14/47/6); this executorship is further evidence of close relationships between the Cabell and Wotton families during the complicated Widecombe property transactions.

In November 1705, Samuel Wotton of Englebourne paid John D'Oyly and his wife Susanna £2,250 and thereby acquired freehold ('lease and release') for the "Manor or Reputed Manor" of Widecombe and those several tenements commonly called Stone, Rowbrookes, Torr, and Hannaford within the Parish of Widecombe-in-the-Moor; existing ongoing life-term tenancies of Bonneyhill tenements (Lower Bonehill) were among numerous properties "excepted" by the appendix to the Indenture (DRO 48/14/8/1a-b). A further £800 in 1707 secured the Manor of Blagdon Pipard (now Blackaton) and Shalloven Meads to Samuel Wotton (DRO 48/14/8/2a-b). So the D'Oyly family was pivotal as ownership of the Dartmoor lordships and properties passed from Richard (4) Cabell to Samuel Wotton,

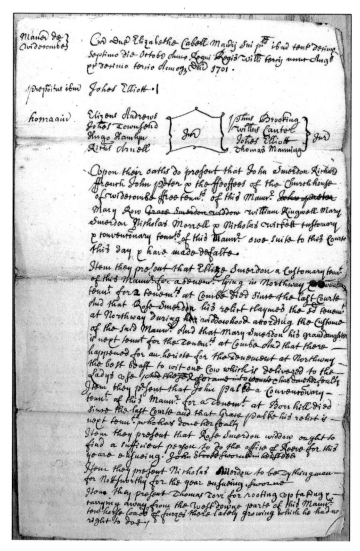

Figure 22. Manor of Widecombe-in-the-Moor Court Roll, 1701 – note Elizabethe Cabell on the first line, reference to John Smerdon, and (near the bottom) the death of John Palk of Bonhill; there is a small amount on a second page. This Court Roll, preserved in the Devon Record Office, Exeter (DRO 48/14/1/15), is reproduced with permission.

via Elizabeth Cabell, Cholmeley, John D'Oyly (and his wife), and then finally to Samuel Wotton. The precise purpose and need of the several transactions remain difficult to deduce; the role of Cholmeley D'Oyly, whom Sandles (2007) described as impecunious when he married Elizabeth Cabell, apparently bigamously (Djabri, 1991), is open to speculation until more details are unearthed.

The Court Roll for 1707 (DRO 48/14/1/16) confirms that Samuel Wotton was then Lord of Widecombe-in-the-Moor. In 1706, he had granted two yeomen the lease of a messuage and a little cottage in Natsworthy with common pasture rights on "Hamildowne and Eastdowne", for the consideration of £120 and one broad piece of gold (DRO 48/14/52/4). Samuel Wotton's ownership of all the Widecombe area properties was finally confirmed by a covenant (to levy a fine) dated 1708 (DRO 48/14/8/3). Later, he acquired the Manor of Spitchwick, becoming its Lord in 1714 (DRO 48/14/41/6a-b; 48/14/2/1-35).

Beside the life leases mentioned above, freehold title to a few other estates was not included in Samuel Wotton's 1705 Widecombe acquisitions. For example, George Leyman assigned all his rights in Stone to Samuel Wotton in May, 1708, "in consideration of £50 and one broad piece of gold" (DRO 48/14/51/8); this farmstead was leased back to Leyman the following day at the annual rent of 5s., and re-leased to him for the same rent in 1728 (DRO 48/14/51/9). The change from Cabell to Wotton lordship is reflected by other documents. For example, the Widecombe messuage of Torr and Belltor leased to Richard Hext in 1676 by Samuel Cabell, for a consideration of £90 and rent of 13s.4d., was re-leased to him by Samuel Wotton in 1731 for £85 and annual rent of 17s.6d. (DRO 48/14/31/2-3).

Ongoing manorial obligations remained with some Widecombe estates for many years. For example, Cabell had demised and granted Lower Barton, east of Bonehill, to William Kingnell in 1685; by indenture in 1704, ownership was transferred to Phillip Brookings, blacksmith. However, in 1740, Jane Aptor (widow and relict of John Aptor, yeoman) did "grant bargain sell assign transfer and set over" this property to John Morrell, subject to an annual rent of 23s.4d. payable to Samuel Wotton's son William and also to the discharging to William Wotton of one third of the herriott or money payable on the death of Kingnell (DRO 48/14/43/10).

In the autumn of 1711, Robert Hannaford, yeoman of Broadaford in Widecombe, acquired a three-lives lease of Bonneyhill and five closes (Northwood, Stone, Barton, Pitts, and Dockwell Meadows) from Samuel Wotton - this was the southern of the two Bonehill farmhouses lying south of the stream, which had formerly been leased to John Polk - the entry price to the lease was £155 and two broad pieces of gold (DRO 48/14/43/3-4); actually, Polk had died in 1701 but his wife, Grace Polk, succeeded him as tenant under John Polk's life tenancy, according to the 1701 Manor of Widecombe Court Roll (Fig. 22; DRO 48/14/1/15). This new 1711 lease was on the lives of John, Robert, and Ivan Hannaford, the annual rent being 31s.5d. (DRO 48/14/139/2). Four years later, in 1715, Samuel Wotton granted a lease to the yeoman John Hannaford on the messuage, shippon, etc., at Bonneyhill, lately in possession of R^d. Tremills, for the consideration of £174 and one broad piece of gold; the annual rent was £12 (DRO 48/14/43/5; DRO 48/14/139/2). This lease was for the northern farmhouse immediately south of the stream (i.e., the current Lower Bonehill farmhouse).

Samuel Wotton granted numerous other leases to properties in Widecombe and Blagdon Pipard Manors between 1716 and 1731, including North Hall Mansion house and two grist mills in 1721 to the yeoman John Andrew (DRO 48/14/47/8). Samuel died in 1735. His Will was dated "on or about" 11th April, 1735 (DRO 48/14/8/5) and his son, William, is recorded as Lord of the Manor of Widecombe in 1735. William's sisters, Dame Mary D'Oyly of Dublin and Susannah Wotton, each inherited £1,000 from their father. In 1736, it was William Wotton who granted John Andrew the renewal of his lease for North Hall Mansion (DRO 48/14/47/9).

William remained Lord of Widecombe until 1742. His Will was probated in 1744 (DRO 48/14/8/4) and in September that year, his brother, Rev. John Wotton of Englebourne, granted a lease on Combe Mead in Widecombe (DRO 48/14/44/9). It was not until January, 1745 that the final Deed (Deed to lead the Uses of a Fine) was signed establishing the Wotton's title (rather than the D'Oyly's title) to the Widecombe and neighbouring properties. This Deed was between "Rev. John Wotton of Englebourne in Harberton, clerke [and] Richard Wotton of Doctors Commons, London, gent., (only sons of Samuel Wotton late of Englebourne, esq., dec'd.)" and Sir John D'Oyly of Oxford, bart. (DRO 48/14/137/8). It included a long list of properties in Rattery, Dartington, Totnes, Holne, Staverton, Harberton, and Widecombe-in-the-Moor; included in the latter were the Manors of Widecombe Town, Spitchwick, and Blagdon Pipard, and messuages called Higher and Lower Natsworthy, Stone, Bonehill, Northway, Southway, etc. For a considerable time, a member of the D'Oyly family continued receiving a legacy from the Manors of Widecombe Town, Blagdon Pipard, and Spitchwick, as evidenced by a receipt to the Wottons dated 1769 (DRO 48/14/8/5).

After William Wotton's death, most Wotton estates, and the Lordship of the Manor of Widecombe-in-the-Moor became vested in Rev. John Wotton. On the latter's death on 5th November, 1746, his Will devised Englebourne along with Spitchwick, Widecombe, and Blagdon Pipard manors, and his other manors and lands in the parishes of Holne, Totnes, Staverton, Dartington and Ashburton, to three trustees (Thomas D'Oyly of Chiselhampton – later Sir Thomas D'Oyly, baronet, John Shapleigh of New Court, Devon, and Rev. Henry Holdsworth; DRO 48/14/8/5) for 99 years, in order for them to raise £2,000 for his only child, Anna Maria Wotton, then an infant only a few months old (Dymond, 1876, pp. 26-27; DRO 48/4/142/4c). John Wotton's Will had a profound affect on Widecombe's future. John's younger brother, Richard Wotton, was Lord of Widecombe Manor from 1747 to 1752. It seems that, subject to the terms of the trust set up under John's Will, any residue of John's estate was to pass to his brother Richard (died 1753) for life and then to Richard's male issue - Richard's only son Samuel died, unmarried and intestate, in 1780 (Dymond, 1876, p. 30; DRO 48/4/142/4c).

Proceedings in the Chancery Court soon ensued to resolve the considerable complications that arose during the three trustees' administration of what had been John Wotton's estates. But one example of the complications was a complex five-party mortgage in 1751 (DRO

48/14/48/12); this included raising £84 for the remainder of the trust's 99-year term on the farmhouse (messuage) and five enclosed fields (closes) called North Meadow, Stone Meadow, Barton Meadow, Pitts Meadow, and Dockwell Meadow, all at Bonneyhill, for John Hannaford (executor of Robert* Hannaford) and Robert Hannaford (son of John* Hannaford and grandson of Robert Hannaford). The similarity of individuals' names and imprecise identification of properties in the preserved legal documents make reconstruction difficult – however, presumably Robert* was late of the southern Bonneyhill farmstead and John* had had the life-time lease of the northern farmhouse; embracing the two Bonneyhills in this mortgage possibly reflects the beginning of their being melded together as a single enterprise (that later became known as Lower Bonehill Farm).

Eventually, at an auction in 1769 decreed by the Chancery Court, the residue of the 99-year term (specified by John Wotton's Will) in the Widecombe and Spitchwick properties and lands was bought for £4,700 by John Dunning, Solicitor General and M.P. for Calne, son of John Dunning of Ashburton (Dymond, 1876, p.27; White, 1850, pp. 453-4; *cf.*, Dame Mary D'oyly's legal testament of 18th April, 1755 - DRO 48/14/8/5). John Dunning built a fine house at Spitchwick for his occasional residence; it was a "neat house" according to White (1850, p. 453).

Three-lives (99-year) leases

One of the first recorded leases in Devon for three lives or 99 years, was that granted by John Southcote to Adam Drewe and his wife in 1545 (DRO 48/14/50/12). Such contracts became the universal mode of leasing tenements and land in Devon for many years. The three lives specified in such leases were usually those of the farmer (the lessee) and two other living people nominated by him – commonly, his spouse and oldest son. A large fine (fee) was charged on initiation of such leases but the annual rent was commonly very small. The names of new lives could replace individuals who had died on payment of an additional fee to the lord of the manor, so some of the leases lasted for more than a century. The long-term security of such arrangements meant leaseholders conducted the farming much like an owner, with a real interest in maintaining and improving the property, at least in the earlier years of a lease. The benefits of the three-lives system caused copyholding to decline rapidly and almost disappear from most of Devon by 1700 (Hoskins, 1954, p. 91). Whether such leases were actually beneficial to tenants and to the land and environment has been much debated. In his detailed review of Devon agriculture, drawn up for the Board of Agriculture and Internal Improvement, Vancouver (1808, pp. 81-4) condemned the mischievous and injurious consequences of 99-year leasing, despite the positive opinion of "some noblemen and gentlemen of the county". He asserted that "Fortunately for the future improvement and prosperity of the country, this species [of tenancy] is becoming much lessened within the last twenty years" (*i.e.*, 1788-1808). His main complaints were that

*is used only to identify which Robert and John is intended.

(a) the same capital investment (as used by tenants to acquire the lease) could have been more profitably used to stock and improve a more-extensive farm rented for a fair annual rent for a short term, and (b) towards the expiry of a 99-year lease (on which tenants had exhausted their capital by the initial high-priced lease purchase), tenants neglected and exhausted the property, which would be offered at public auction upon termination of the lease (*cf.*, Hoskins, 1954, p. 92). The system was replaced slowly, but continued in places until the end of the 19th century.

Status of yeomen
Relative social status was of tremendous significance in 16th and particularly the 17th and 18th century rural England. It is important that many of the farmers in Bonehill hamlet were documented as yeoman, especially because in the Widecombe area there were few resident gentry and the lords of the manors were all essentially absentee. Although no particular type of land tenure was essential to be called a yeoman, all those called yeomen were primarily occupied with the land and its interests. Any person engaging in trade or business which became more important than farming was no longer termed yeoman, but was called baker, blacksmith, joiner, etc. (Campbell, 1983, p. 26). Yeomen comprised a substantial rural middle class in England between knights and gentry above them, and husbandmen and labourers below them; the social rank tended to carry numerous onerous obligations to serve in parish life and administration.

Yeoman, being a descriptive rather than a legal term, was used somewhat loosely. According to Campbell (1983, pp. 25, 61, 64), the fact that yeomen's

> lands were their own, or directly under their control, bred in them a sense of pride and personal interest and responsibility, not discernable nor to be expected in the poorer husbandmen or tenant farmers who worked at somebody else's bidding and had often to struggle too hard to make ends meet to derive much pleasure from the lands they labored on.

Farmsteads held under three-lives leases (99-year leases) were worked and developed under the control of the 'three lives' who owned the leases; several yeomen in Bonehill held their farm under such a lease.

Campbell noted that the favourable position of yeomen in England under Queen Elizabeth and her immediate successors was referred to by almost every contemporary writing about the social structure of the age. Certainly, Risdon writing in 1714 (1811, pp. 10-1), and others' contemporary accounts of Devon, did so vigorously.

Campbell (1983, pp. 99-101) named yeomen in many parts of eastern and southeastern England between 1576-1620 who bought or exchanged very small parcels of land (often only 1 or 2 acres) to consolidate a contiguous holding; it is not improbable that similar practices occurred on Dartmoor to create small fields from original strips worked or owned by various farmers. Before the aratral field walls were built in Bonehill, the adjacent contour-controlled field strips were likely to have been owned/worked by different people. At some stage, sale, or quite probably exchange, of small parcels of land could have allowed contiguous strips to be enclosed within aratral walls/hedges by a single owner. The Bonehill tenements that developed were all very compact farms of contiguous fields until the end of the 19th century.

Because John Smerdon was cited as yeoman in a marriage settlement of 1733, it is not unlikely that his predecessors at Middle Bonehill Farm also had yeoman status. The name John Smerdon was cited as yeoman in the Friends of Devon Archives' (2007) lists of Widecombe freeholders for 1733, 1762, and 1771, and specifically as freeholder in 1762; these lists are of those owning freehold or copyhold land worth £10 per year or more, and who were qualified for jury service. These lists of freeholders show there were 17 Widecombe-in-the-Moor yeomen in 1733. The Smerdons and numerous other Bonehill (Bonneyhill) leaseholders who were yeomen must have had considerable local status and have been obvious leaders in their community.

A note on units of area measurement

A note explaining the meaning of rods, poles, and perches referred to in Chapter 1, which along with roods, are frequently cited in Chapter 4 for farmstead sizes, etc. Although largely obsolete today, these units were all used well into the 20th century, as even pre-World War II school children will confirm; the units can be somewhat confusing because all could either be measures of length or of area. Also, although standardised in 18th to early-20th century use, centuries ago the units tended to be of dissimilar size in different regions of Britain.

Originally, 1 acre was 1 furlong long and 4 rods (poles or perches) wide (*i.e.*, 22 yards wide, 1 rod being 16½ feet = 5½ yards = 5.029 meters). 1 furlong is ⅛ of a statute mile (as still widely used in horse racing today). 1 acre is 0.40466 hectares (ha) and 1 statute mile is 1.609 kilometres (km). Until recently, the size of farmsteads was commonly expressed in acres, roods, and (square) poles, abbreviated to *a. r. p.* (see Fig. 32). 1 acre = 4 roods = 160 (square) poles = 0.4047 hectares. So, since 1 acre is 4,840 square yards, 1 square pole is 30.25 square yards, and a square pole is an area measuring 1 pole by 1 pole (*i.e.*, 16.5 feet x 16.5 feet = 30.25 square yards). Expressed differently, there are 4 roods to an acre, and 40 square poles (rods or perches) to a rood, so a (square) pole is one 160th of an acre = 0.00625 acres.

In Chapter 4, *a.* = acre, *r.* = rood, and *p.* = (square) poles (rods or perches).

Today, around Widecombe, all people think of field sizes in terms of acres (as shown on current Ordnance Survey maps) although currently, for government purposes (*e.g.*, reports to Natural England or Defra – Department for Environment Food and Rural Affairs), land must be recorded and reported in terms of hectares only.

4

BONEHILL (OR BUNHILL) HAMLET THE MID-17TH TO 21ST CENTURIES

The romantic setting of Bonehill hamlet was captured on the first page of Eden Phillpotts' (1913) novel, *Widecombe Fair*, where an Exeter gentleman and young Tryphena Harvey, sitting on the lower slopes of Bel Tor one February, looked southwest towards the Webburn Valley and Widecombe; on

> their left stood the pile of granite known as Bone Hill Rocks, and beneath them, separated from the Moor by a wood of pine and larch, lay Bone Hill Farm, a dwelling with a cheerful face that turned towards the south.

Thornhill Lane, the old Natsworthy to Ashburton horse and wagon trail following the 1,100 foot [335.5m] contour on the open moor below Bel Tor, immediately above the old curving aratral granite-walled fields, still yields the best view of Bonehill hamlet today (Fig. 2). Of course, in 1913, Bonehill hamlet comprised several farms with at least three ancient farmsteads, namely Lower Bonehill, Middle Bonehill, and Upper Bonehill (*cf.*, Whitten, 1998); Lower Bonehill comprised two tenements in the 18th century. The Phillpott's quote probably referred primarily to Middle Bonehill farmstead, although the newly re-thatched Higher Bonehill house and barn are the most obvious buildings from Thornhill Lane today. During the 17th and 18th centuries, Widecombe yeomen and farmers developed great independence because, unusually by comparison with other parts of Devon and England as a whole, the lords of the nearby manors were absentees and not greatly concerned with local affairs (*cf.*, Woods, 1977, p. 18). Even by the end of the 19th century, Baring-Gould (1899, p. 246) related that

> Widecombe is a valley shut in by moor; where the people are much of a law to themselves, having no resident manorial lords over them, and having no neighbours. A sturdy and headstrong race has grown up there, doing what is right in their own eyes, and somewhat indifferent to the opinions and feelings of the outer world. In winter they are as much closed in as was Noah in the ark . . . Widecombe is walled up to heaven on the west by Hameldon [Hamel Down], and the morning sun is excluded by a bold chain of tors on the east.

As Beeson and Masterman (1979, p. *x*) noted

> there have always been occupations besides farming in Widecombe. The census for 1841 mentions miners, millers, shoemakers, tailors, farriers, and masons among others. There was a flourishing wool industry with a fulling mill well into the 18th century. Today disruption of the old community is caused not so much by the fact that fewer people derive a living from farming,

but because improved communication by road encourages more people to derive a living from outside the parish.

From the moorland of Bonehill Down (documented as Bunhildowne in 1652 and 1668 and Bunhill Downe in 1676; DRO 48/14/51/4-6), the present road crosses a track, Thornhill Lane, and passes between the granite hanging and latching posts of the original Bonehill Gate (Fig. 23). An actual gate seems not to have been there in living memory so, today, commoners' stock (cattle, sheep and ponies) put out to graze on the Moor often roam down the lane to Widecombe-in-the-Moor's village green. Amongst Devon villages, Widecombe is unusual in possessing a green and a square, which was the focus of the medieval village; both show clearly on the 1843 Tithe Map (Fig. 24). From the 'gate', the lane descends a steep hill, 1-in-5 in places, to the granite houses and barns of Bonehill (Bunhill) hamlet, just over half a mile (1 km) east of St. Pancras church at the heart of Widecombe. Gawne and Sanders (1998, pp. 4 & 38) asserted that:

Figure 23. Road through Bonehill Gate from the open Moor by Bonehill Rocks leading down to Bonehill hamlet; the walls are built with the abundant local granite boulders (field stone). Large holly trees flank the road, along with gorse and last-year's bracken. The hog's back of Hamel Down forms the western horizon across the West Webburn River valley, January 2009.

> Almost every one of the present Widecombe farms was mentioned in tax or other records before the year 1400, and a number of them much earlier... The tin industry flourished on the Moor from the mid-12th century, reaching a peak in the late 15th and the 16th centuries... At this time many of the surviving longhouses were built... Bonehill is one of the most interesting of the Widecombe clusters of farms. It is mentioned in the 16th century Court Rolls of Widecombe Town Manor... but the settlement must be more ancient than that. The buildings are arranged very much like those of the deserted Hound Tor settlement, though much further apart.

'A. Moorman' (Dymond, 1875, p. 3) fulminated about incorrect Ordnance Survey place-name orthography; Bunhill (not Bonehill or Bonhill) was frequently used in 19th century documents and, because it appears in numerous places throughout Dymond's (1876) book, it was probably the accepted name used by the gentry when he was writing. Bonneyhill (and several variants) was widely used in earlier legal documents. Many ideas about the meaning of Bonehill have been mooted, but none seems really justified. It could be suggested that Bunhill is an ancient inheritance from Irish invaders/colonists, since 'bun chnoic' in Irish Gaelic are the foothills, but this spelling does not appear in the oldest preserved documents. Kelly's Directories changed from Bunhill to Bonehill only after 1923.

The old roads to Bonehill and Widecombe-in-the-Moor

Bonehill hamlet with its winding single-track metalled road, without sign posts at either end, is still considered very isolated by many of today's city dwellers. As noted in Chapter 2,

Figure 24. Centre of Widecombe-in-the-Moor in 1843. St. Pancras church (surrounded by the cemetery) is shaded, but browny-pink unlike the other buildings; G = the Green (crossed by the road) immediately north of the church; S = the small square is just to the southwest. Adjacent fields show Tithe Map field numbers; brown creases show from original map, in which north was towards the top left. The East Webburn River, flowing southwest, is crossed by the road to Widecombe Hill (near NE corner of map). From the Commissioners' copy of the Tithe Map preserved in the Devon Record Office, Exeter; image reproduced with permission from the digitisation produced by DRO in 2008.

Donn's (1765) map is basically very accurate about this general area, but it yielded little information about access to Widecombe, and Bonehill is not shown. Little evidence remains today of the sole road to Widecombe mapped by Donn (Fig. 21), which descended from east of Bonehill Rocks to the bottom of today's Widecombe Hill (near the recently built Upper Northway Farm). It would be interesting to determine when the present main road down Widecombe Hill was first defined, and whether Donn's map truly reflects the situation in 1765.

In the mid-18th century, there must have been considerable flux into and out from Widecombe-in-the-Moor by local people and by visitors travelling on horse-back or on foot. The Parish Officers' Accounts show that, on eight occasions between 1711 and 1727, small payments (*e.g.*, 6*d.**) were given to licensed beggars (both men and women) who came to Widecombe with a pass, signed by one or more justices, because they had suffered some disaster (fire, flood, shipwreck, etc.) and were unable to find ways of maintaining themselves. It was agreed at a 1727 Parish Meeting that parishoners would not pay for anything given to travellers asking alms, but this embargo was lifted some two decades later (Woods, 1977, p. 17), and one finds 2*s.*6*d.* reimbursed to the Overseers for a payment to 12 travellers in 1749, who were said to be travelling home after release from Turkish captivity. Interestingly, vermin carried a much higher price. Thus, in 1736, the bounty paid out of Poor Rates was 5*s.* for every fox and vixen able to prey for themselves (and 2*s.*6*d.* for every young cub unable to take prey for itself) taken or killed within the parish and hung in the parish tree. Badgers were valued at only 1*s.* (Woods, 1977, p. 19).

For centuries, packhorses were the only method of transporting goods throughout Devon; strings of packhorses were not generally replaced by wheeled carts, etc. until about 1800 and, on Dartmoor, carts must have been very rare until well into the 19th century (*cf.*, Groves, 1970, p. 186). That Arthur Aptor, yeoman of Widecombe, bequeathed Arthur, his grandson, £5 and the wheels of his wain in 1659 (Woods, 2000, p. 113) reflects the novelty and value of wheels at that time; Woods noted Aptor also owned land in Ashburton, so

*d being a penny and s a shilling; 6d. = £0.025 in the current decimalised currency; 1s. = £0.05; 2s. 6d. = £0.125; 5s. = £0.25.

possibly his wain was used mainly off the Moor. In the absence of hedges and fences, bridle tracks probably changed course frequently as weather conditions and changes in land ownership dictated (*cf.*, Moreland and Bannister, 1993, p. 25). It was said there were only three or four very blind roads across Dartmoor in 1786 (Simpson, quoted by Groves, 1970, p. 194). Vancouver (1808, pp. 370-1) confirmed the paucity of wheeled carriages throughout Devon, and provided colourful descriptions of the perilous nature of Devon's much-frequented country roads, especially when a traveller meets with, or is overtaken by, a gang of pack-horses:

> The rapidity with which these animals descend the hills, when not loaded, and the utter impossibility of passing loaded ones, require that the utmost caution should be used in keeping out of the way of the one, and exertion in keeping a-head of the other.

Hoskins (1954, p.152) cited Carrington's 1840 report that there were no carts in Bridford (between Christow and Moretonhampstead) in 1800, although there were some 50 in that Parish by 1840. Strings of packhorses for transporting goods were not generally replaced by wheeled vehicles in Devon until about 1800 and, on Dartmoor, the latter were probably rare well into the 19th century (Groves, 1970, p.186). Baring-Gould (1912, p. 9) recalled

> It was not so long ago that an old man in Sheepstor died who could remember the first cart coming into the village. Before that everything was brought on pack-horses.

Baring-Gould (1890, p. 215) described how massive blocks of granite could be moved with a truckamuck, that is by a horse placed between the trunks of two young trees, the tops of which were fastened to the animals while the roots dragged on the ground. Very large pieces of granite would be levered onto these roots and dragged along. Apparently, for the heaviest loads, four trees were used with the middle ones lashed together. Sometimes, an additional horse in front would help pull very heavy loads and, for steep hills and rough ground, oxen shod with iron cues, Q's, were used instead of horses (quoted by Hoskins, 1954, p. 150, and Sheldon, 1928).

The first printed Ordnance Survey map covering Bonehill (Old Series, one inch to one mile Tavistock Sheet XXV; *i.e.*, scale of 1: 63,360), issued in 1809, was based on 1802-3 drawings; Margary (1977, plate 34) included a facsimile of this map. Although important parts of Devon were surveyed at 3 inches or 6 inches to the mile, the Widecombe area was surveyed only at 2 inches to the mile (1:31,680) due to economic pressures on the Board of Ordnance during the Napoleonic invasion threats. Much of the surveying around Widecombe may have been done by cadets in training (Harley, J. B., and O'Donoghue, Y., *in* Margary, 1977, p. xvi, *et seq.*). On this map, the roads entering and leaving Widecombe are similar to those of today, except for Bonehill Lane; the extant track running northwards between Middle and Higher Bonehill farmhouses towards Wooder was shown clearly. Bonehill Lane below Bonehill Gate was correctly shown terminating between the farmsteads, but no route down to the village was depicted (despite a small northwards spur off the main Widecombe Hill road shown just west of Northway Bridge over the East Webburn

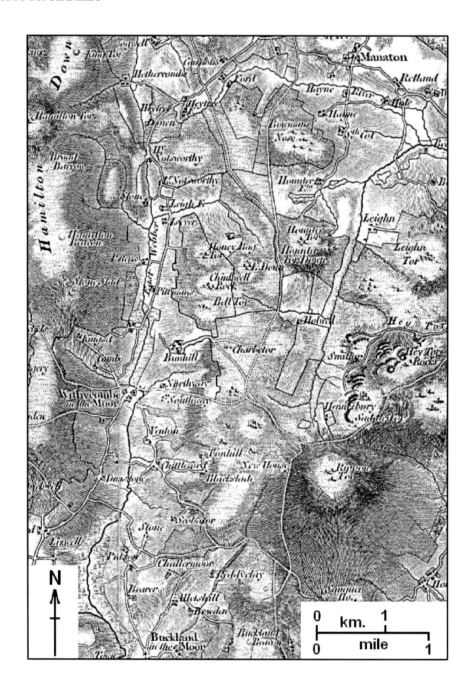

Figure 25. Small part of Ordnance Survey Sheet XXV 1:63,360 map based on surveying of 1802-7 and issued initially in 1809; this Figure shows State 6 printed closer to 1885 with revisions, but the changes were mainly railways to Princetown, etc., beyond the margins of this image. The original heavy hill shading (hachures) on this Series of maps made it very difficult to read other detail in the hilly regions.

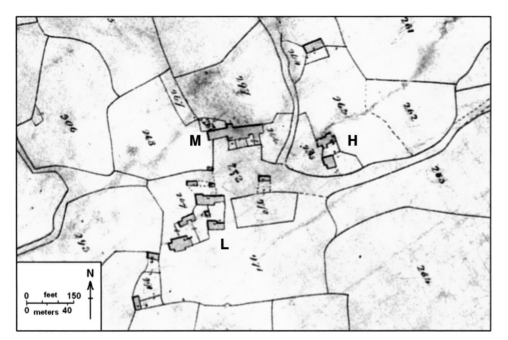

Figure 26. Bonehill hamlet in 1843; this map does not show the stream, which is now crossed by a bridge southwest of Higher Bonehill Farm. L = Lower, M = Middle, and H = Higher Bonehill farmsteads. Note the house and barns at Middle Bonehill are attached. Some walls shown south of Lower Bonehill farmhouse have now disappeared and the waste (labelled 271) is open to Bonehill Lane, descending from the east from the open Moor. From the Commissioners' copy of the Tithe Map preserved in the Devon Record Office, Exeter; image reproduced with permission from the digitisation produced by DRO in 2008.

River). Figure 25 is a small part of the sixth state of this 1806 black-and-white map with its strong hachure hill shading; this map, published by Lᵗ Colˡ Mudge, was engraved at the "Drawing Room in the Tower by Benjⁿ Baker & Afsistants – The writing by Ebenʳ Bourne." Bunhill is near the centre of Figure 25; note the spelling of Withycombe *in the* Moor, Hamilton Down, and Hey Tor Rocks – undoubtedly, such spelling stemmed from phonetic renditions by surveyors who questioned local residents about the names of prominent landscape features before 1802.

The 1843 Tithe Map also showed Bonehill Lane, descending from the open Moor, terminating between Lower and Middle Bonehill farmsteads (Figs. 26 and 27). However, that map also showed a well-defined walled route down to a bridge across the East Webburn River, and thence to the bottom of Widecombe hill; this routeway was accessed by a gate in the southwest corner of the yard around Lower Bonehill farmhouse (Fig. 26). The East Webburn River is shown well on the Tithe Map (Fig. 27), but it had a wholly fictitious course on the printed Ordnance map (Fig. 25). Indeed, the whole area between Bonehill hamlet and St. Pancras Church appears to have been sketched in the drawing office, without reference to the actual topography. Enlargements of this part of the 1809 O.S map and a part of the more accurate Tithe Map are shown in Figure 28; in the former map, the river under Northway Bridge flows from the northeast, rather than being the main East Webburn River coming from the north. The lower part of Bonehill Lane was omitted from successive

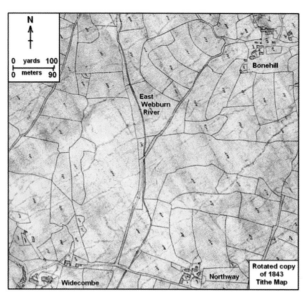

Figure 27. Widecombe-in-the-Moor to Bonehill hamlet in 1843. Note Bonehill Lane is interrupted by the hamlet; there is a gate across the lane immediately north of where is crosses the long east-west field boundary. From the Commissioners' copy of the Tithe Map preserved in the Devon Record Office, Exeter; image reproduced with permission from the digitisation produced by DRO in 2008.

Ordnance Survey revisions up to that of 1885 (printed by electrotype in 1888). The differing pattern of the fields on either side of this lane reflects a distinct boundary, which would probably have been an ancient footpath that was improved early in 19th century. In addition to the northwards spur (immediately west of Northway Bridge as if to Bonehill), the Ordnance Survey also showed another spur (through the 'o' of Northway – see Fig. 28), which may have been the site of the road shown on Donn's map (Fig. 21).

Maintenance of Bonehill Lane from just west of "Northway Bridge to Bunhill Down Gate" (7 furlongs 4 yards; 1.41 km) in 1864-72, and the blowing (blasting) of 46 feet (14 m) of rock in Bunhill Lane at 6d. per foot in 1803, are recorded in an original notebook (Woods, 2000, pp. 108, 113). The 1896 Ordnance Survey revision (New Series, 1 inch/1 mile Sheet 338, published 1900) showed Bonehill Lane extending all the way from Bonehill Gate to the present-day main road.

Prosperous times for Devon farmers during the Napoleonic Wars (ca. 1793-1815) were followed by very lean years in the 1820s and following decades. It would appear that conditions were improving in the Widecombe area by 1850 because the first documented Widecombe Fair, a cattle fair, was held that year. There is some confusion about details; the Fair programme for 2003 (Widecombe Fair, 2003, p. 37) stated *Woolman's Exeter and Plymouth Gazette* for 19th October, 1850 announced a fair would be held on Friday 25th October, 1850 and on 2nd November it reported that, for the first time, a fair had been held on Tuesday 29th October, 1850. Citing the newspaper, the programme reported:

> there was a large attendance of yeoman [*sic*] and gentlemen of the district and good business was done. It was thought that the Fair should be permanently established. 736 sheep were penned, 75 score and 7 fatted beasts plus 4 bulls. One South Devon cow, reared by the Vicar Rev J H Mason, was sold for £15. 10s. About 50 ponies were driven in, the breed and character of the Widecombe stock being highly appreciated. ... It was agreed that Widecombe was fortunate to have a Green that was an ideal site, also that it could have a Free Fair.

The *National Gazette of Great Britain and Ireland* for 1868 reported a fair is held annually on the third Thursday in October, while *Morris and Co's Commercial Directory and Gazetteer* for 1870

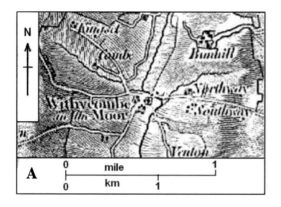

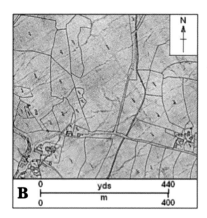

Figure 28. Comparison of Tithe Map and Ordnance Survey versions of the topography between Widecombe-in-the-Moor and Bonehill hamlet.
A. Ordnance Survey map: Erroneous rivers and topography on of the 1809 edition O.S map (State 6 issued until about 1880); detail from map in Fig. 24. Note the tortuous course of East Webburn River north of Withycombe in the Moor, and the hill spur extending south-westwards from Bunhill.
B. Tithe Map: Detail from Fig. 27 showing the correct course of the East Webburn River. From the Commissioners' copy of the Tithe Map preserved in the Devon Record Office, Exeter; image reproduced with permission from the digitisation produced by DRO in 2008.

recorded a Cattle Fair is held annually on the second Tuesday of September. According to Hoskins (1954, p. 87) the landed classes across Devon were at the height of their opulence and political influence in 1873, and there was no depression in farming at that time. The sale of stock ceased at Widecombe Fair by the latter part of the 20th century, the event having become a country fair held every second Tuesday in September. As beautifully described and illustrated by the Widecombe and District Local History Group (2007), the annual fair continues annually on that same day.

Middle and Higher Bonehill farmhouses face south and the lane and stream, while Lower Bonehill farmhouse is south of the lane and stream; all these farmhouses are well protected by rising ground, except to the west. The stream rises in Beltor Mire (just southeast of Bel Tor and north of Bonehill Rocks), descends (just north of the lane) to Bonehill hamlet (*cf.* Hemery, 1983, p. 654), passes beneath a small road bridge and then on into Lower Bonehill; it eventually joins the East Webburn River; in the driest years, this stream tends to disappear by Lower Bonehill farmhouse during the summer months.

Middle Bonehill Farm

Middle Bonehill farmhouse is a traditional longhouse with cross passage; the ground plan (see Fig. 34) and front elevation were illustrated by Gawne and Sanders (1998, p. 40). The thatched porch (with window above) is a later, photogenic, addition (*e.g.*, Woods, 1988, p. 129; Gawne and Sanders, 1998, front cover and pp. 27 & 40). Beeson and Masterman (1979, p. 10, *et seq.*) stated the house roof is thatched and undoubtedly it was originally; however, a photograph published in 1983 (Hemery, 1983, Fig. 318) showed the western half (over the traditional byre) roofed with a corrugated material and the main house (eastern half) roofed with black-coated pegged slates; the timbers under the slates were found to be not very old when examined for the owners in the 21st century by Mark Hutchins. The byre

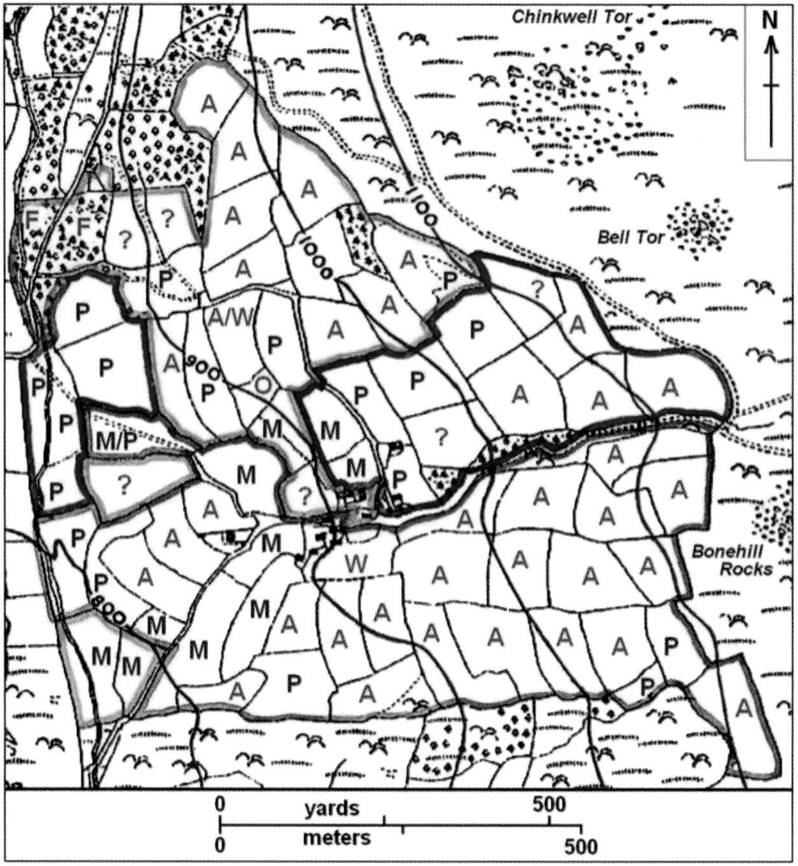

Figure 29. Field use in Bonehill hamlet in 1843, showing Higher (red outline), Middle (green outline), and Lower (blue outline) Bonehill Farms. In this and other detailed maps of Bonehill, field outlines and contours based mainly on the O.S. 6 inch/1 mile (1:10,560) map *Devonshire Sheet C. S.W.* surveyed in 1884, second edition (1906).

A = arable; P = pasture; M = meadow; O = orchard; F = fir plantation; W = waste; ? = unknown.

retains the massive granite-slab floor, central drain, and other original features. The farmhouse and its huge detached threshing barn are both Grade II* listed buildings because of special architectural and/or historic interest; the traditional byre at the western end of the house was noted especially in the listing. However, the ground plan of Middle Bonehill farmhouse on the Tithe map (Fig. 26) shows a single connected set of buildings. Clearly, alterations occurred after 1843 making the threshing barn wholly separate from the farmhouse; it is unknown whether the removed portion was merely an open linhay or a more substantial structure. Gawne and Sanders (1998, p. 28) suggested the threshing barn "..is likely to be the longest in Widecombe (37'6) [11.43 m]." The small barn south of the road, but north of the stream, was sold by Jason Mitchell and Sally Lodge (then owners of Middle Bonehill) to Joan Perkins (then owner of Bonehill Bungalow) in 1992. At that time, this small barn had a tallet (hayloft) with braith floor of brushwood laid on loose hedge poles across the beams (*cf.*, Havinden and Wilkinson, 1970, p. 178); shortly thereafter, the tallet was removed when the corrugated-iron roof was replaced with slate.

A considerable part of the land comprising Middle Bonehill Farm was arable in 1843 (Fig. 29); the names of the farm's fields are shown in Figure 30 and Table 3. From early times, every field on Dartmoor had a name; most were self-explanatory. Several fields shown in Figure 30 are called Lears which, according to Hemery (1983, p. 68), referred to a locality selected and used for depasturing animals. Hemery (1983, p. 94) suggested the use of waste for a small enclosed area of rough pasture was peculiar to south Dartmoor; however, the term was quite widely used across the county for the open moorlands until the late 19th century, although not necessarily for small enclosures.

Beeson & Masterman's (1979) list of Middle Bonehill fields (derived from the 1843 Tithe Map) contained a few typographical errors, *viz.*: (a) parcel 266 Fir Plot appears to be 256 (now field O.S. 7957), a plot of old larches, etc., currently part of Higher Bonehill's land, (b) field 300 cannot been identified, (c) field 322 was also listed under Higher Bonehill (where it is correctly recorded), and (d) field 325 (now 2453) was omitted. Beeson and Masterman's (1979) list (after omitting 256, 300, and 322, and adding 325) amounted to 48.408 acres (see Table 3). At auction in 1869, Middle Bonehill Farm was described as 48*a*. 0*r*. 31*p*. (= 48.194 acres or 19.50 ha), sold as 21 acres of meadow & pasture, *ca.* 21 acres of arable, and *ca.* 6.408 acres plantation. Some fields were still arable in 1949 (Table 1), but all are now to permanent pasture, although a couple of big old apple trees remain in the old orchard (Fig. 30(17)). Most of these fields are now owned and farmed by a local farmer who lives in another part of Widecombe. Much of Moory Meadow (Fig. 30(22)) was converted into a large pond late in the 20th century.

Early history of Middle Bonehill

Brown (1998a, A, p. 9 & C, pp. 14-5) compiled a useful history of Smerdon ownership of Middle Bonehill. He reported John Smerdon (JS0) lived at "Bonehill" and, amongst other children, his sons Richard (RS1) and Sidwell were born in 1572 and 1576, respectively; nothing is known of his social status or in which specific Bonehill farmstead he lived. Because Richard Cabell purchased Middle Bonehill in 1658 as part of the Widecombe estates, it is probable that John Southcote owned Middle Bonehill farmstead back in 1570 and had the farmhouse built there before his death in 1585. To avoid confusion, the successive generations of John Smerdons are referred to here as JS0, JS1, JS2, ... (see Table 4); similarly the Richard Smerdons are identified by RS1, RS2, ...

Regular Widecombe routine was rudely disturbed on Sunday, 21st October, 1638 by a great storm, in the middle of which, the crowded church was struck by lightning during Rev. George Lyde's sermon. The death and injury to the congregation and the structural

Current O.S. field number	Field Name	Acres	1843 use	1949 use	Old O.S. field number	Tithe map number
5549	House, garden & yard	0.400	arable	building	715	267
3500	Yonder Broadlands	2.020	arable	arable	650	244
4100	Great Broadlands	2.398	arable	arable	662	245
4600	Yonder Creeping All	2.588	arable	pasture & furze	663	246
5183	Homer Creeping All	1.960	arable	arable	670	247
5685	Homer Creeping All	0.878	arable	plantation	669	248
6382	Higher Furze Park	1.990	arable	arable	{667	249
6880	Higher Furze Park	0.940	pasture	furze	{667	250
5975	Lower Furze Park	1.900	arable	pasture	668	259(a)
5272	Round Park	1.960	arable	arable	671	259(a)
4851	Little Meadow	1.150		pasture	714	268
4572	Granite Piece	1.770	pasture	meadow	672	301
3972	Lower Granite Piece	1.985	arable	meadow	673	302 & 303
4164	Orchard	0.740	orchard	pasture	712	304
4559	Yonder Meadow	1.474	meadow	meadow	713	305
2966	Lower Winter Lears	2.110	arable	arable	709	318
2028 & 1526	Tongue Meadow	3.900	meadow	meadow	780	333
3466	Winter Lears	2.080	pasture	meadow	710	308
4081	Little Broad Lears	1.550	arable	pasture	674	309
3988	Middle Broad Lears	2.240	arable	arable	675	310
?	Stone Field	2.953	?	arable	676 & 677	311
2453	Moory Meadow	2.350	?	meadow	706	325
?	Higher Plantation	2.002	fir	NOT in Farm	681	316
2779	Stouts	2.470	pasture	NOT in Farm	678	317
1177	Little Plantation	0.620	meadow	NOT in Farm	680	321
?	Plantation	1.544	fir	NOT in Farm	682?	349

Table 3. Middle Bonehill Farm fields in 1843 and 1949

N.B.: 1 acre = 0.4047 hectares; three-digit field numbers refer to those on the 19th century series 1:2,500 (25-inch/mile) Ordnance Survey maps and the four-digit numbers to those on the newer Revised Series O.S. maps.

damage to the church have been retold many times. Brown's (1998b) realistic but fictional account of the day's events was written around many members of the extended Smerdon family who were undoubtedly all involved intimately in the shocking event.

According to Brown (1998a), some 70 years after Richard Smerdon's (RS1) birth (with at least one intervening generation), John Smerdon (JS2) married Margaret in about 1641. The oldest of their five children, John (JS3), was born on 12th December, 1641, and married in about 1682. Brown suggested that, although there is no known documentary evidence, the inheritance line indicates John (JS3) owned Middle Bonehill.

Lower Barton and Middle Bonehill (presumably) were amongst numerous estates referred to in a schedule (annexed to the Indenture for Richard Cabell's purchase of Widecombe-in-the-Moor properties from Sir Courtney Pole in 1658); the schedule listed properties

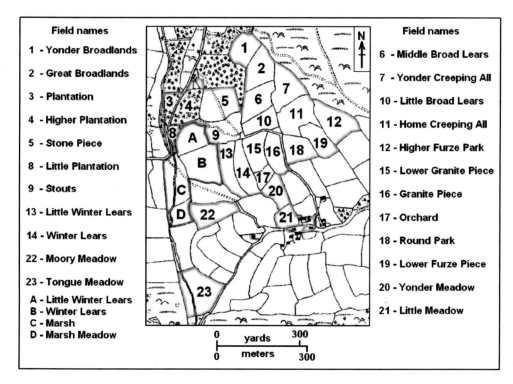

Field names

1 - Yonder Broadlands
2 - Great Broadlands
3 - Plantation
4 - Higher Plantation
5 - Stone Piece
8 - Little Plantation
9 - Stouts
13 - Little Winter Lears
14 - Winter Lears
22 - Moory Meadow
23 - Tongue Meadow
A - Little Winter Lears
B - Winter Lears
C - Marsh
D - Marsh Meadow

Field names

6 - Middle Broad Lears
7 - Yonder Creeping All
10 - Little Broad Lears
11 - Home Creeping All
12 - Higher Furze Park
15 - Lower Granite Piece
16 - Granite Piece
17 - Orchard
18 - Round Park
19 - Lower Furze Piece
20 - Yonder Meadow
21 - Little Meadow

Figure 30. Middle Bonehill Farm field names in 1843 edged in green. Four Higher Bonehill Farm fields edged in red.

"excluded" because the occupiers had previously been granted 99-year (three-lives) leases by the Lord of the Manor (DRO 48/14/7/7a), *viz*:

> One Estate of Ric[d] Smerdon of 99 years in a certain parcel of land called the Lower Barton determinable upon his own death the reversion thereof granted to Ric[d] his son for the same term determinable upon his death.....

> One Estate of Arthur Smerdon in one Tenement in Bonehill [*sic*] for 99 years determinable upon his own death The Reversion is granted to John his son for the life term determinable upon his death

This 'Bonehill' is almost certainly Middle Bonehill.

According to the fourth line of an Indenture of 1689 confirming Cabell's lease of Bonneyhill (what is now Lower Bonehill farmhouse) for three-lives to William Cauntor, the property was lately occupied by John Smerdon, freeholder of Bonneyhill (DRO 48/14/43/2). Because all Bonehill farmsteads were commonly referred to as Bonneyhill in the 1680s, it is difficult to be certain which farmhouse Arthur Smerdon (in 1658) and John Smerdon (before 1689) occupied, and whether this John Smerdon holding a freehold in 1689 was JS3 or another; John Smerdon is a very common name. The two Bonneyhill tenements south of the stream were only combined as Lower Bonehill Farm some years later.

Table 4. Some John Smerdons of Middle Bonehill

1641   John Smerdon (2) married Margaret.

        John Smerdon (3) born 12.12.1641 and died 19.5.1708.

1658   Arthur Smerdon tenant with three-lives lease when Richard Cabell acquired
        Lordship of Widecombe.

        John Smerdon (4) born 18.2.1682.   yeoman

1689   John Smerdon (? 3), **freeholder** of Bonneyhill cited as former occupier in
        Cauntor's Bonneyhill lease.

        John Smerdon (5) born 11.3.1704.   yeoman

1762   John Smerdon recorded as a **freeholder**.

        John Smerdon (6) born 17.9.1747 died 17.9.1807   yeoman

1809   John Smerdon unencumbered owner.

        John Smerdon (7) born 1.11.1773 died 25.5.1853.   yeoman

        John Smerdon (8) born 24.1.1811.

1869   Middle Bonehill sold at auction by John Smerdon (8).

Although Brown (1998a) claimed successive John Smerdons and their families are known to have been living at Middle Bonehill Farm since the mid-1570s, the legal documents of 1658 and 1689 make this an unsafe conclusion. Although John Smerdon ownership (possibly deeply mortgaged) and yeoman status in 1570 are just possible, it may be more likely that the early Smerdons were customary tenants, holding the land according to the custom of John Southcote's manor (? North Hall).

Brown recorded that John's (JS3's) son John (JS4) was born on 18th February, 1682; "I S 1682" is incised clearly into the granite of Middle Bonehill farmhouse's 'new' porch (*i.e.*, signifying [I]John Smerdon 1682); this must mean JS3 lived at Middle Bonehill in 1682, which compounds the question about the freehold in 1689, referred to above (see Fig. 31). John (JS4) married Jane *ca.* 1704 (Brown, 1998a, A, p. 9; C, p. 14) and he (as a yeoman) and his wife Jane were recorded in a marriage settlement dated 21st April, 1733 [DRO 3555M – 0/T/7/34]. John's (JS4) oldest son, John (JS5), born on 11th March, 1704, and baptised at St. Pancras Church (Hemery, 1983, p. 655) that year, married Anne in about 1742. Their older boy John (JS6), born in 1747, married Joan Stockman in April 1772, and died in 1807.

Thus, when the Smerdon's originally acquired the freehold to Middle Bonehill is uncertain. As noted in Chapter 3, John Smerdon (JS6) was cited as a yeoman in the Friends of Devon Archives' (2007) lists of Widecombe freeholders for 1733, 1762, and 1771, and specifically as freeholder in 1762. These lists of freeholders show there were 17 yeomen living in Widecombe-in-the-Moor in 1733. The Widecombe History Group (2004) showed that John

Smerdon (JS6) was one of the overseers of the Poor in Widecombe for many years, being cited as examiner on 17 Indentures for children between late 1759 and autumn 1799; he was a church warden in 1788. Another John Smerdon (JS7), born on 1st November, 1773, inherited the farmstead on his father's (JS6) death in 1807.

In 1808, there were 102 houses occupied by families and 9 vacant houses in the Parish of Widecombe; including children, the total population was 1,043 (515 male; 528 female) with 745 engaged in agriculture, 5 in manufacturing, and 293 in other occupations (Vancouver, 1808, p. 415). There was a friendly society in Widecombe with 40 members; members of such societies commonly paid small monthly dues and received weekly payments when unable to work because of sickness. Vancouver (1808, p. 110, note *o*) claimed of such societies

> There is no one thing that contributes so essentially to the relief of the parish burthens, or tends more to preserve the independent spirit of the peasantry, and should therefore be countenanced and promoted by every regular and prudent means as generally as possible.

The Widecombe Poor Rate and other Parochial Taxes, assessed at 3*s*.9*d*. in the Pound (£ of land value), raised £388.15*s*.2¼*d*., and Vancouver (1808, p. 111) cited the annual expenditures as:

Expended on the poor (not in any workhouse, etc.)	£281. 3*s*. 2*d*.
Law suites, removal of paupers, Overseers expenses, etc.	£ 31. 2*s*. 4¼*d*.
Other expenses, church, highways, bridges, militia rate, etc.	£ 30. 16*s*. 9¾*d*.

Anonymous old notes on the copy of Beeson and Masterman (1979, p. 11) in Widecombe Parish Chest record that, at the 1841 Census, John Smerdon (JS7) farmer 65, his wife Martha (neé Tremills, age 55), and their 3 children lived at Middle Bonehill (along with John Miller, agricultural labourer, and three apprentices, Elizabeth Harding age 15, Thomas Squires age

Figure 31. Architectural drawing of front (south) elevation of Middle Bonehill farmhouse by Elizabeth Gawne (died 1992). Walls and trees prevent the entire elevation being viewed from any one place; note "IS 1682" carved in porch granite lintel. (Reproduced from Gawne and Sanders, 1998, p. 40).

Table 5. – John Smerdon's (JS7's) indentured workers at Middle Bonehill farmstead
(data from Widecombe History Group, 2004)

Name	Date of Indenture	Age at Indenture	Occupation	Indenture until	Pay	Doc.Folio number
Mary French	21.10.1789	?	husbandman	marriage or 21 years	food, drink, apparel	255
Samuel Warren (1816)	6.12.1799	?	husbandman	21 years	meat, drink, apparel, etc.	471
John Andrews	22.4.1791	?	husbandman	21 years	meat, drink, etc.	504
Ann Cleave	29.5.1804	8	housewifery	21 years	board, lodgings, etc.	264
George Eascott	16.10.1801	9	husbandman	21 years	board, lodgings	304
Elias Smerdon Leaman	18.6.1810	8	husbandman	21 years	meat, drink, etc.	552
Hanna Hext	1. 9.1815	9	housewifery	marriage or 21 years	meat, drink, etc.	402
Richard Harvey	7.5.1827	14	husbandman	21 years	board, lodgings	365
John Harvey	31.8.1830	10	husbandman	21 years	food, drink, clothes, lodging, washing	029
Elizabeth Turner	14.6.1826	11	husbandman	marriage or 21 years	meat, drink, etc.	531

N.B. Because of the commonness of the name John Smerdon, the Widecombe History Group (2004, folio 471) recognised there is some question whether Samuel Warren actually worked in Middle Bonehill or was indentured to another Smerdon in Ashburton.

15, and Ellen French age 10). The 1845 Tithe Apportionment cited the same ownership/occupancy of the 48a. 0r. 31p. (Brown, 1997, p. 13). A major part of the farm's land was arable in 1843 (Table 3; Fig. 29). By the time of the 1851 Census, John Smerdon (JS7) and his wife Martha (aged 77 and 65), sons John (JS8) 40, Richard (RS2) 30, Lawrence 24, and Edwin 24, and grandson Albert Norris age 4, along with agricultural labourers Robert King (23 from Ugborough) and William Warren (20 from Buckland), and general servants Martha Lee (22 from Widecombe) and Mary Hart (14) were all recorded as living at Middle Bonehill. John and Martha's other children were Nancy S (born 1809), William (born 1813), Betsy (born 1819), and Herbert (born 1827) according to Brown (1998a, A, p. 9).

Like his father, John Smerdon (JS7) was an Overseer of the Poor and was one of the examiners on 24 Indentures for children from 1811 to October 1829. The Widecombe History Group (2004) referred to 'John Smerdon (junior)', presumably John Smerdon (JS7) of Middle Bonehill Farm, as living and farming at 'Bunhill', and being the employer of numerous indentured young people over the years (see Table 5).

The indenture system was clearly well established by 1790 and comparable numbers of young boys and girls must have lived at, and been employed by, most of the Parish's farms over the preceding century or more. Widecombe History Group's (2004) data file (based on 572 documents preserved in The Widecombe Parish Chest) details the indentured employees within Widecombe over about half a century. Vancouver (1808, p. 259), in his thorough review of Devon agriculture and rural employment at the very beginning of the 19th century, was very positive about the system of indentured servants operated under a 1600 Elizabethan Act of Parliament. He considered that, on balance, the system was good and useful and, being more prevalent in Devon than other counties, should be more widely adopted across England. He recognised, however, the need for some changes. The original Act "subjects the occupier of 10*l.* per annum [a farmstead worth £10 per annum] to the receiving regularly in turn, a parish apprentice"; Vancouver (1808, pp. 360-1) wrote that currently, due to inflation,

> magistrates will rarely submit to the imposing of an apprentice where the occupation amounts to less than 20*l.* per annum; still in these days, and where there is often a house full of children to nurse and provide for, even this standard of liability seems to press too hard, and to require a farther extension.

> The manner too in which the females are sometimes treated, requires that some farther regulations should be made to soften the severity of their servitude. Scraping the roads, lanes, and yards, turning over mixings and filling dung-pots, is at best but a waste of time, and a feeble effort of infantile strength. What can a female child at the age of ten or twelve years be expected to perform with a mattock or shovel? or how will she be able to poise, at the end of a dung-fork, any reasonable weight, so as to lift it into the dung-pots slung upon the horses' backs, for packing out the manure to the distant parts of the farm? Even driving the horses after they are loaded, is by no means an employment proper for such girls, being altogether incompatible with the household and more domestic duties they ought early to be made acquainted with.

> Nothing can fairly be urged against the treatment of the boys, whose instruction and services are rendered more suitable, and better understood: their morals are better cultivated and more strictly preserved than there could be any reasonable chance of expecting from their remaining at home. Boys so trained and instructed, are uniformly found to make the best servants, and to prove the steadiest and best labourers afterwards; but the girls, too frequently, from an early dislike to their avocations, and in which they well know they are not hereafter to be continued, cannot well be supposed to have much emulation or desire to excel in them; hence premature connexions are formed, and which by marriage terminates their servitude, but without their having acquired in it those domestic qualifications upon which the comfort of a peasant family so essentially depend.

As mentioned above, John Smerdon (JS7) inherited Middle Bonehill Farm in 1807, owning it until he died on 25th May, 1853, aged 79 (Brown, 1998a, C, p. 13), when John Smerdon (JS8) inherited the farmstead. So, John Smerdon (JS7) and his son (JS8) undoubtedly attended the first Widecombe Fair in 1850.

John Smerdon's (JS7) Will, dated 16th April, 1853, was probated on 9th December, 1853; total effects were sworn to be less than £800 (Mason Tucker Solicitor's Papers, Devon Record Office, 924B/F4/14*). He had bequeathed "the parlour and bedchamber above the same" in his Bunhill (Middle Bonehill) house to his wife Martha (neé Tremills), with the use of the household furniture belonging to those rooms, for her life; she died some 23 years later on 29th December, 1876. Martha was also left (a) the bonus (but not the principal sum assured) on her husband's West of England Assurance Office assurance policy, and (b) an

---

*A copy of the Will in the Probate (kindly provided by Peter Smerdon in 2002) has 'sons' in bold type – should it have been 'son'? Possibly not, as John's (JS7) mother's maiden name was Stockman.

Figure 32. Poster advertising the auction of Middle Bonehill Farm on 19th June, 1869.

annuity of £10 per annum to be paid half-yearly in arrears out of his Bunhill properties. These bequests had to be accepted and taken by Martha in lieu and full satisfaction of all 'dower and Thirds'; failing this, she was to have no benefit under the Will. The messuage and premises of Middle Bonehill were left to John (JS8) and his heirs and assigns forever, subject to the bequests to Martha and £300 to Richard (RS2) and £50 (out of his personal property) to his son William, both of the latter to be paid two years after his (JS7's) death. Out of the assurance policy, £200 was bequeathed to JS7's daughter Betsy; his "sons Herbert, Edwin Stockman and Lawrence Stockman" were to share all the rest of his personal property equally within 12 months of his decease. John (JS8) was instructed to discharge all of the deceased's debts out of the messuage.

According to Brown (1998a, A, p. 9, & C, p. 13), John (JS8) and Richard (RS2) Smerdon shared Middle Bonehill after their father (JS7) died, but Brown did not define "shared"*. In 1863, Richard Smerdon (probably RS2) of Bunhill, yeoman, was served notice to make repairs to buildings on Pitton estate, just to the north (DRO 3555 M-1/E9).

Following the Napoleonic Wars, the 1820s to 1840s were very lean years for Devon farmers generally, and Middle Bonehill had been inherited by John Smerdon (JS8) shortly afterwards in late 1853. Sixteen years after his father died, Middle Bonehill farmstead was offered at auction by John Smerdon (JS8). The Contract of Sale and a poster (Fig. 32) advertising the auction (both sold at a Tavistock auction in the 1990s) provide details of the John Smerdon family over the preceding 60 years. This Contract recorded that an old declaration (extant in 1869) attested John Smerdon (JS7) owned Middle Bonehill unencumbered in about 1809. The sale closing was specified for

*John Smerdon (JS8) also inherited Merrivale Newtake (Parish of Whitchurch) from his father (JS7) and occupied it in the 1840s; he and his brother Richard (RS2) contested the Wills of Richard (RS3) and Nicholas Smerdon, all of whom shared the same great grand-father, John Smerdon (JS4) of Middle Bonehill (Brown, 1998a, C, p. 14).

noon on 27th December, 1869; despite an unidentified tenant at Middle Bonehill, the purchaser was to be entitled to possession of such parts of the premises as were in hand and to the rents for the let parts from 25th December, 1869 onwards.

The vendor (JS8) at the 1869 auction had sold as mortgagee; the mortgage and release had been effected in October, 1831, because £200 had been lent to John Smerdon (JS7) by Richard Honywill. The auction-sale document shows the Middle Bonehill buildings were insured for only £200 up to 25th December, 1869. However, the entire estate apparently sold for £2,050 (implying the substantial sum of £1,850 for roughly 48 acres of land, if the buildings were really only worth the insured value of £200). After the auction, a £250 deposit was paid and acknowledged by signature (over a 6d. stamp) by Wm. K. Kennaway, Tucker & Son, Agent for the Vendor, who attested he had "... this day purchased the before mentioned messuage farm and lands".

On the back of the actual auction-sale document, bidding was recorded in pencil as:

Bidding

| Mr. Hooper | £1600 | 1660 | 1700 | 1720 | 1750 | 1770 | 1800 | 1820 | 1850 | 1870 |
| Mr Rd Smerdon | £1650 | 1670 | 1710 | 1730 | 1760 | 1780 | 1810 | 1830 | 1860 | 1880 |

| Mr. Hooper | 1900 | 1920 | 1940 | 1960 | 2000 | 2020 | 2050 |
| Mr Rd Smerdon | 1910 | 1930 | 1950 | 1970 | 2100 | 2030 |

The unsuccessful bidder, Richard Smerdon (presumably RS2), was possibly the unnamed tenant mentioned in the closing documents. The pencil notes also include a list of Encumbrances on Bunhill totalling £2,300 (significantly more than the sale price); the figures are clear, but the descriptions of the items are almost illegible, although they include £1,200 plus £200 interest owed to Mr. xxx (illegible name ?), £300 plus £72 interest owed to R. Smerdon (? RS2; possibly the original bequest due from his father, JS7), and £250 plus £34 interest owed to R. (?)Tucker. Separately listed (and possibly also owed) are:

Land Tax			£1. 3. 0	
Tithe	£1. 9. 2			
	£3. 6. 5			
	£4. 15. 7	say	4. 12. 0	
			£5. 15. 0	
Poor Rates	£1. 10. 6			

The signature of Wm. K. Kennaway, Agent for the Vendor and purchaser, is unexplained but suggests that a Mr. Hooper may have been bidding on Mr. Kennaway's behalf.

By 1881, the Census listed George Hannaford (40, born in Widecombe), his wife Susanah (45, from Manaton), their three sons William (17), Albert H. (15), Louis J. (11), daughter

Mary E. (6), and their nephew Martin Northcott (11, born Christow) all living at Middle Bonehill. Hemery (1983, p. 674) noted "... this family of yeomen still farmed at Bonehill (George [Hannaford]),..." in 1880.

Although Gawne and Sanders (1998, p. 41) claimed that:

> According to the Parish Rate Books and to papers in the Ashburton Museum, a series of John Smerdons farmed at Middle Bonehill till the 1850s, and the farm was owned by members of the Smerdon family until the beginning of the 20th century,

as shown, the property was actually bought by Wm. K. Kennaway at auction in 1869.

John Smerdon (JS8) of Bunhill was listed in the P.O. Directory of Devon (1856, p. 334) and in Kelly (1866, p.1059), but the only Smerdon recorded by Kelly (1873, pp. 424-5) in Bunhill was Edwin Smerdon of Bunhill Villa, although a Richard Smerdon was cited as Bunhill farmer in Harrod's Directory (1878, pp. 732-3) without mention of which farm. By the 1881 Census, Richard Smerdon (presumably RS2) unmarried, age 65, with occupation listed merely as "income from land and houses", was living with his unmarried brother Edwin (age 54), "farmer of 75 acres", at Bonehill Villa, a newly built house just west of Middle Bonehill (see Fig. 35). No Smerdons, except Edwin, were listed as owners or occupiers of Bunhill property in the 1890 Widecombe Poor Rate Register; one of the four who signed that Register's Declaration was Edwin Smerdon, Churchwarden.

The four plantation fields 316, 317, 321, and 349 (total 6.636 acres, see Table 3), shown on the Tithe Map, apparently comprised Item 46 of the 1890 Widecombe Poor Rate Register (*6a. 2r. 19p.* = 6.62 acres) belonging to, and occupied by, Wm. **H.** Kennaway (possibly a mistake for Wm. **K.** Kennaway). The 48.408 acres auctioned in 1869, less these 6.636 acres, comprise the 41.772 acres at Middle Bonehill listed as house and land owned by Wm. **H.** Kennaway and occupied by George Hannaford in Entry 28 of the 1890 Poor Rate Register. Actually, the Register recorded the slightly higher *43a. 0r. 31p.* (43.194 acres); acreages calculated from Tithe data (Table 3) as listed by Beeson & Masterman (1979) and used at the auction, are low for some purposes, because they do not include the roads and verges which had been assigned old (but not new) Ordnance Survey individual measured acreages and field numbers, that were included when Commoners' Rights, etc. were calculated and recorded at Devon County Hall.

Alexander Nelson Radcliffe acquired Middle Bonehill Farm on 29th April, 1909 by Conveyance on Sale from William Kennaway, who was exercising

> powers of a tenant for life under the Settlement created by the Will of Mark Kennaway recited in the said Conveyance [29.4.09] and under the Settled Land Acts notwithstanding anything contained in an Indenture dated the 26th June 1877, recited in the said Conveyance

When later sold at auction on 19th October, 1949, as part of Radcliffe's (deceased) Bagpark Estate, the sale particulars listed Middle Bonehill Farm as 41.772 acres (*i.e.*, precisely the 1869 auctioned amount less the plantations later acquired by Mr. Kennaway); the sale particulars referred only to the enclosed fields, not lanes, verges, etc.

John Nosworthy occupied Middle Bonehill as tenant from at least 1910 until at least 1935 (Kelly, 1910, p. 805; 1923; 1926; 1930; 1933; 1935). John Nosworthy "for Bunhill" was present at the Widecombe Town Manor Beating of the Bounds on 25th September, 1909 (cited by Brewer, 2002, p. 82 with photocopy of H. H. Hannaford's 1909 Diary). By 1939, Kelly (1939, pp. 840-1) showed Jas. Ford occupying Middle Bonehill; according to Hemery (1983, p. 655), he was a descendant of the 16th century Fords of Bagtor House. At the 1949 auction of the Radcliffe estate, Middle Bonehill was sold (as rented by Jas. Ford) for £1,925 (according to a pencil note on the late Ned. Northmore's copy of the auction catalogue). The Fords owned Middle Bonehill Farm and, in 1983, Hemery (p. 655) recorded that Jim Ford, then farming on a more restricted scale, still kept "... old traditions alive, including the use of horse-power for mowing and general farm haulage." Hemery (1983, Fig. 319 on p. 633) included a photograph of the farmhouse and the horse-drawn cart, which was said to be in daily use.

It is understood from verbal comments that, under her Will, the widow Mrs. Ford left her farm to a medical charity, which put the entire property up for auction - a sufficient bid not being found for the whole, the farmhouse, barns, and one field were sold as one lot, and all remaining land as another, except for Moory Meadow (O.S. field 2453, 2.35 acres) which lies northwest of Bonehill House. Title to Moory Meadow was acquired by Robin Palmes who constructed a large lake in the 1980s. The small stream in the field (O.S. 2459) to the north was diverted for the lake's water supply, and the lake shows clearly on the Ordnance Survey (2005) Outdoor Leisure Series 1:25,000 map, Sheet 28.

In 1989, Middle Bonehill was owned by Jason Mitchell and Sally Lodge, who lived there with their two children. As noted above, the small traditional barn south of the road was sold in 1992 to the owner of Bonehill Bungalow. In 1992-3, Jason Mitchell and his family moved away, Middle Bonehill being purchased by Bob Spiers and Sophie Richardson (Mrs. Sophie Cuthbertson); Sophie's daughter (by her first marriage), Coral Cuthbertson, lived with them. After Bob and Sophie's marriage their daughter, Sienna, was born in 1996, being the first baby actually born in Bonehill hamlet for many decades. Later, the field immediately north of the farmhouse, Home Meadow O.S. 5554, was purchased from the current owner of Higher Bonehill Farm. Sophie and her daughters continued living at Middle Bonehill farmhouse until November 2006, when the property was sold on the open market, apparently for £635,000. Bob Spiers died towards the end of 2008. The elaborate leat system in Yonder Meadow and Little Meadow (O.S. 25 inch/1 mile mile map SX7177, fields 4559 and 4851) was restored by the current owners.

Lower Bonehill Farm

Lower Bonehill farmhouse is a traditional Dartmoor granite longhouse, rubble built in a particularly massive style (Fig. 33); although of late middle-16th century origin, many

Fig. 33. North and West elevations of Lower Bonehill farmhouse, October 2007.

extant features are 17th or younger, as shown by Figure 34. A 20th century, pre-restoration, elevation drawing by Elizabeth Gawne was reproduced in Gawne and Sanders (1998, p. 43). Gawne's contention that Lower Bonehill tenement predates Middle and Higher Bonehill farmsteads is certainly correct. Gawne and Sanders' (1998, p. 44) noted there

> is not a great deal left to show the age of this house, but from the large corner stones, the general proportions and the slightly tapering plan, it would be reasonable to think that it was built during the second half of the 16th century.

The house originally had a thick thatched roof, which accounts for the shape of the main chimney stack above the present slate roof. Figure 34 allows ground plans of Lower and Middle Bonehill Farmhouses to be compared; the details are based on Gawne's original measurements and drawings on a copy of her Lower Bonehill plan (in the author's possession since 1989) and in Gawne and Saunders' (1998, pp. 40 and 43) illustrations. Many features of Lower Bonehill's central passage are intact, including a series of enormous ashlar (dressed) 17th century granite blocks lining its east side; the late Ned Northmore recalled shearing sheep in this cross passage, long before the oak staircase was installed in about 1987. A fine granite fireplace backs onto this wall; Hemery (1983, p. 654) noted "its lintel eight feet long and 2 feet 9 inches deep, the underside 4 feet 3 inches above the hearth stone" (2.44 m x 0.84 m, 1.30 m) . His Figure 14 (p. 21) is a poor photograph of the fireplace and bread oven to the right, which Gawne and Saunders (1998, p. 44) considered to have been added after the chimney was built, because of its "uneven projection". The bread oven in

Middle Bonehill Farmhouse is also on the right; some archaeologists have suggested that such ovens are customarily on the left side of the fire. A granite staircase, said to have been against the north wall (see Fig. 34), has long since disappeared.

There are now five granite outbuildings. The only trace of the sixth building shown on the Tithe Map (see Figs. 26 and 35(7)) is the southern wall near its south-western corner, now visible in a field-boundary wall. Each of the six extant buildings was listed by the Secretary of State as buildings of special architectural or historical interest (Grade II) on 3rd November, 1986 under the Town and Country Planning (Listed Buildings and Buildings in Conservation Areas) Regulations 1972, set up under the Town and Country Planning Act, 1971, Section 54.

According to Beeson and Masterman (1979, p.11), Gawne believed that, because of

> an excessive number of out buildings belonging to Lower Bonehill by comparison with Higher and Middle Bonehill, it is a fair assumption that one of them was once the dwelling house of the fourth [Bonehill] tenement.

In fact, numerous, documents evidence that, prior to 1800, what is now Lower Bonehill comprised two tenements, both referred to as Bonneyhill and leased to different tenants. Actually, two extant barns (Fig. 35 (2) and (4)) have features suggesting they might originally have been dwellings - long-houses with a cross passage.

The current farmhouse (Fig. 35(1)), having been tenanted almost since time out of mind, was apparently in extremely poor repair by the 1930s and was condemned; after a new bungalow (Bonehill Bungalow, Fig. 35 (BB)) was built for the tenant in 1935, the farmhouse was only used as a byre. According to legend, Uncle Frank, the tenant Frank Nosworthy, would sit in front of the fire in winter with his feet on a block of granite to keep them clear of water; this is wholly believable because a good spring further up the lane (close to the lane in field O.S. 8049), which originally supplied all of Bonehill hamlet's drinking water, still flowed in a pipe under the new Bonehill Bungalow (to the east) until capped by Percy Bishop in the 1980s; *via* lead piping, this spring still serves Middle Bonehill and unused easements are in place for supply to Bonehill House. Eventually, the roof of Lower Bonehill farmhouse caved in. A painting dated September 1972 by D. F. Daw (of 14 Newton Road, Bishopsteignton) shows the thatch had been replaced by slate before the collapse (presumably in 1920-21, see below). The painting (Fig. 36) shows bushes inside the upper end of the derelict house, and three young sycamore trees, one of which still thrives north of the house. The farmhouse

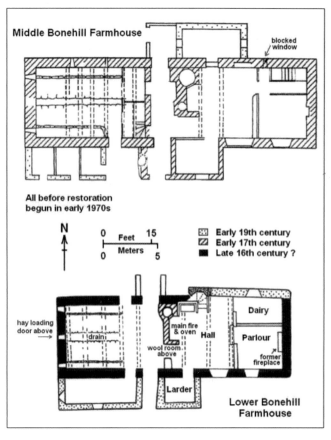

Figure 34. Ground plans of Middle and Lower Bonehill Farmhouses based on originals prepared by Elizabeth Gawne (see text). Adapted from reproductions in Gawne and Saunders (1998, pp. 40 and 43).

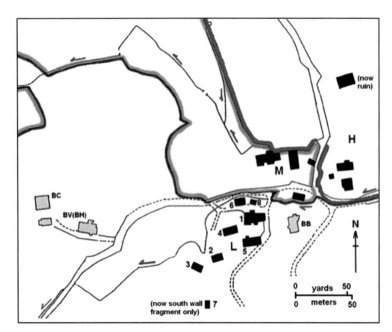

Figure 35. Bunhill hamlet farmsteads and recent houses and bungalows.
Original farmsteads in 1843 (black):
L – Lower Bonehill fields (blue boundary); see text for numbered buildings.
M – Middle Bonehill fields (green boundary);
H – Higher Bonehill fields (red boundary).
Newer houses and bungalows (grey):
BV(BH) – Bunhill Villa (more recently known as Bonehill House);
BB – Bonehill Bungalow;
BC – Bonehill Cottage.
Green arrows indicate stream and leat flow directions.

remained derelict until bought by Mr. and Mrs. Scott on 17th October, 1972, when renovations began; it is said the new owners initially camped inside the ruins.

The original byre of Lower Bonehill farmhouse comprised, as usual, the lower (western) end of the longhouse; unusually, the byre had a separate entrance in the north wall (which is now a window). On the west elevation, large windows were installed in about 1980 and the hung Delabole slate (damp protection) in 1995 (Fig. 33). Few obvious signs of the fireplace in the middle of the east wall of the house remain, although a prominent chimney stack (now sealed off) survives; a fireplace arch remains in the upstairs east wall, but the chimney cavity within the wall extends down to a lower level - a ventilation brick into it was installed in 1995, when the chimney was more securely sealed against water ingress. The original granite paving of the farmhouse byre was re-laid in what is apparently the fourth ancient Bonehill longhouse (Fig. 35(2)) by Tom Nosworthy before April 1974 (according to a letter from Malcolm Scott to Elizabeth Gawne). The present long kitchen, against the south wall of the original farmhouse byre, was an early 19th century addition (Gawne and Saunders, 1998, p. 43); instead of the usual rubble between granite walls, the cavity of the kitchen is filled with concrete - a feature said to be a hallmark of Tom Nosworthy's rebuilding work in the early 1970s (*pers. cmmn*, Pam Nosworthy, 2003).

The eastern end of the original fourth Bonehill tenement (Fig. 35(2)) no longer survives, but in 1843 the building was much longer than now as shown by the Tithe Map (Fig. 26). There is a blocked-up doorway in the present eastern gable of this building and, beside this (on the outside), an orthostat, which probably remains from an open-hearth fireplace; another blocked-up doorway, in the present south wall, suggests there had been a central passage between the original, but now missing, living quarters and a byre, which survives and is now floored with the granite slabs moved from the main farmhouse. West of this building, a small granite byre (Fig. 35(3)) is built into the sloping ground; it also has an orthostat against the exterior eastern gable, beneath the door servicing the hay loft for the stalls beneath.

A further massive barn (Fig. 35(4)) between the remains of the fourth tenement and the present house might have been yet another longhouse. As is common (and like the present house), this building is aligned east-west and set into ground which rises to the east, so the eastern gable-end is about half the height of the western one; the possible cross passage lay south to north. Beeson and Masterman, 1979, p. 11, *et seq.*) asserted the western gable of this building exhibits two different types of masonry, as if a chimney had been removed, and the gap replaced with much more worked stone approaching the degree of dressing of the older parts of St. Pancreas Church in Widecombe. On the side of this newer part is a dressed stone window casement

Figure 36. Painting of Lower Bonehill Farmhouse in September 1972 by D. F. Daw.

These features are well preserved (see Fig. 37). During restorations in 1991, a further window casement was exposed temporarily, high at the west end of the north wall. Questions remain about these features, because a byre would normally have been at the west (downhill) end of a longhouse, and not be equipped with windows and a fire place. In 2004, the eastern end of this building was renovated with a new doorway, level with the ground to the east.

The other two listed granite barns at Lower Bonehill are:
(a) a small stables (Fig. 35(6)) immediately northwest of the present house, with hayloft above and an access door high in the eastern gable. This compact building (Fig. 38) was originally used for the work horses and, although now roofed with corrugated iron, was undoubtedly thatched initially; original unglazed window slits are built into all four walls.
(b) a large east-west barn (Fig. 39 and Fig. 35(5)) south of the house, with wide doors facing each other in the north and south walls, and only one window (in the east gable); the dirt floor was cemented over in the early 1990s.

Adjacent to the former stables are remains of an ancient linhay (Fig. 35(8)) which must have been used for cart storage, etc.; only the huge granite boulders of the north wall and three orthostats on the south side remain. The late Harold Cole said there had originally been a thatch roof; now, with a corrugated iron roof, the linhay serves for storage.

Figure 37. Worked stone in the western wall of the barn shown as 4 in Fig. 35; in the distance is the slated barn 5 of Fig. 35.

Early history of Lower Bonehill

Bonehill and Widecombe-area history to the late 17th century was reviewed in Chapters 2 and 3. Lower Bonehill farmhouse (Fig. 35(1)) was apparently built in the late mid-16th century during the Southcote family's ownership of extensive Widecombe properties. Originally, what is now Lower Bonehill comprised two farmsteads, both known as Bonneyhill, amalgamated by the beginning of the 19th century. It is unknown whether John Southcote himself commissioned these expensive granite buildings, or who lived in and worked the farmsteads initially. The Southcote estates may not have included Middle Bonehill, although its earliest occupants may have been Southcote tenants. The 1745 Deed detailing the Wotton Estates had specifically mentioned Bonehill (probably meaning the two tenements that later became Lower Bonehill).

Figure 38. (above) Old work-horse stables shown as building 6 in Fig. 35; note external steps (single boulders protruding from wall) to the hay loft on eastern gable.

Figure 39. (right) Large barn (building 5 in Fig. 35) south of Lower Bonehill farmhouse viewed from northwest (August, 2001); note small kennel on north wall and extension along west face used for chickens at one time.

At auction in 1769 decreed by the Chancery Court following Rev. John Wotton's death, the residue of the 99-year trust for Widecombe and Spitchwick properties and lands was bought by John Dunning for £4,700 (see Chapter 3 and Table 6). Some years later, John Dunning was created Baron Ashburton of Ashburton (Fig. 40) in March, 1782 by George III and, on 31st March that year, he married Elizabeth Baring of Larkbear, Exeter. Unhappily, he died of paralysis on 18th August, 1783, aged only 51. His son, Richard Barré Dunning (born 20th September, 1782) inherited his father's title, estates, and fortune; in numerous genealogical websites, his birth date is stated wrongly as 1752.

Numerous documents between 1803 and 1818 record the granting of leases for various farmsteads and other properties in Widecombe by the second Lord Ashburton (see Table 7); these leases obviously confirm Lord Ashburton's ownership of the estates (*cf.*, Rennells, 1999).

It is important that the 1803 14-year lease of Bonehill, from Lady Day 1804, refers to "All those two messuages or tenements situated at or called Bonehill" now occupied by Thomas Hannaford; this clearly means the whole of the combined Lower Bonehill Farmstead. The seven- year renewal of Thomas Hannaford's Lower Bonehill lease from Lady Day 1818 was more specific than any preceding documents about the property, *viz*:

> All that messuage tenement and farm called Bonehill together with an overland tenement called Lower Barton All situate in the said Parish of Widecombe in the Moor and containing in all about eighty seven acres ... now in possession of Thomas Hannaford...

These leases also imply that both of the two Bonneyhill farmsteads were included in the 1769 Court-mandated auction, and Gawne and Sanders (1998, p. 39) were correct in writing that

Table 6. Bonehill and Widecombe: some ownership and occupation details since 1750

1762: John Smerdon cited as freeholder at Middle Bonehill farmstead.

1769: John Dunning, MP (Solicitor General, MP for Calne) bought (at auction) main Widecombe and Spitchwick estates for remainder of the 99-year trust established for the late Rev. John Wotton's estates.

1782: John Dunning created Baron Ashburton.

1783: Richard Barré Dunning, Second Baron Ashburton, inherited Widecombe, etc. estates on death of his father.

1803 & 1807: Thomas Hannaford, yeoman, renewed lease of Bonehill (Lower Bonehill).

1809: John Smerdon was unencumbered owner of Middle Bonehill.

1823 (15 Feb.): Miss Margaret Baring inherited the Widecombe properties on death of Second Lord Ashburton; Thomas and William Hannaford, yeomen, leased Bonehill farm (Lower Bonehill).

1825; Thomas and William Hannaford acquired lease for Lower Bonehill.

1841-1845: William and Nancy Hannaford + 7 children occupied Lower Bonehill farmstead.

1845: After reversion following expiry of 99-year Wotton trust, Lower Bonehill and many other Widecombe properties inherited by Rev. Thomas Fry, who became Lord of Widecombe-in-the-Moor Manor.

1860: John Wotton's properties held by Court of Chancery (following Rev. Fry's death on 27 March 1860).

1867: Auction of Wotton's properties by order of Court of Chancery; Mrs. Caroline Mason Drake (neé Brodrick) bought North Hall and Lordship of Widecombe; undetermined buyer of Lower Bonehill Farm.

1869: Middle Bonehill Farm sold at auction by John Smerdon.

1873-5: Richard Rowe, farmer, occupier of Lower Bunhill Farm, presumably as tenant.

1881: George Hannaford and family occupied Middle Bonehill.

1890: Andrew Windeatt was owner of Lower Bonehill Farm; Peter Hannaford was the occupier.

1909: A. N. Radcliffe acquired Middle Bonehill from William Kennaway.

1910: Frank Nosworthy tenant of Lower Bonehill Farm from at least 1910 until 1972.

1910: John Nosworthy tenant of Middle Bonehill until at least 1935.

1919 (18 June): Michelmore, Loveys & Sons offered Lower Bonehill Farm at auction (unsold).

1920 (25 March): Alexander Nelson Radcliffe bought Lower Bonehill and made new lease for tenant Frank Nosworthy.

1935: Lower Bonehill farmhouse condemned and Bonehill Bungalow built for the tenant, Frank Nosworthy.

By 1939: Jas. Ford tenant of Middle Bonehill.

1949 (Oct.): At auction, Radcliffe's executors offered Lower Bonehill (unsold) & Middle Bonehill (sold as tenanted).

1950 (17 Feb.): Francis Hamlyn bought Lower Bonehill Farm from Radcliffe's executors; Jas. Ford owner of Middle Bonehill.

1953 (26 Oct.): Jasper Thomas French bought Lower Bonehill on death of Francis Hamlyn.

1971 (21 Nov.): Jasper French died; Frank Nosworthy's Lower Bonehill tenancy ended in 1972, Linda Tremaine Nosworthy and Phyllis Thirza French sold the farmstead as the inheritors.

1972 (19 Oct.): William Wallace Whitley of Holwell (Lower Bonehill Purchaser); Malcolm and Joyce Margaret Phyllis Scott of Basingstoke acquired the buildings and limited adjacent land; Mr Pearson (of Ipswich) and Mr Rothman (of Winchester) acquired the 9.49 acres by Bonehill Rocks. Joan Perkins bought Bonehill Bungalow from Wallace Whitley.

1974 (14 Oct.): Malcolm Scott died.

1976 (22 March): John Sydney Charles Smith and Georgina Ann Smith of Cambridgeshire, bought (from the 1972 sub-purchasers) and occupied Lower Bonehill farmstead (including *ca.* 15.5 acres land).

1980 (22 June): Anthony Victor Smith and Betty Kathleen Smith bought and occupied Lower Bonehill Farm.

1986 (March): Neil Godfrey and Leila Esther Godfrey from London bought Lower Bonehill as holiday home.

Before 1989: Middle Bonehill owned by Jason Mitchell and Sally Lodge.

1990 (June): present owners bought and occupied Lower Bonehill Farm.

1992: Bob Spiers and Sophie Richardson acquired Middle Bonehill, but moved away and sold to present owners in 2006.

Figure 40. First Lord Ashburton by Sir J. Reynolds (from Baring-Gould, 1899).

Doc. Date	Property	Tenant	Rent	DRO document
	Table 7. – Some of the leases granted on Richard Barré's, second Lord Ashburton's, Widecombe properties.			
17. 9.1803	Bonehill	Thomas Hannaford (yeoman)	£69 15s.	48/14/43/6
20. 9.1803	Higher Natsworthy, messuage	Shadrach French (yeoman)	£30	48/14/52/8
20.12.1803	North Hall mills, field & garden	John Tremills (miller)	£21	48/14/47/10
20.12.1803	Messuage of Stone	John White (yeoman)	£30	48/14/51/10
20.12.1803	Broadaford	Richard Hannaford (yeoman)	£120	48/14/13/1
20.12.1803	Lower Natsworthy, messuage	George Norrish (yeoman)	£28	48/14/52/9
20.12.1803	Coombe, Southcombe, etc.	John Hannaford (yeoman)	£100	48/14/46/3
20. 3.1812	Tenement called Northall	Richard Brooking (yeoman)	£54 4s. 6d.	48/14/47/11
25.10.1817	Messuage of Stone (40 acres)	John White (yeoman)	£36	48/14/51/11
25.10.1817	Bonehill & Lower Barton	Thomas Hannaford (yeoman)	£90	48/14/43/7
13.11.1817	Broadaford (180 acres)	Richard Hannaford (yeoman)	£105	48/14/13/2
18.11.1817	North Hall mills, field & garden	John Tremills (miller)	£21	48/14/47/12
1. 3.1818	Coomb, South Coomb, Hamlyn's Northway, etc.	Thomas Hannaford (yeoman) & John Hannaford (yeoman)	£105	48/14/46/4
	Leases granted by Anne Selby, Lady Ashburton (after Lord Ashburton's death)			
13.11.1823	Broadaford (180 acres)	Richard Hannaford (yeoman)	£100	48/14/13/3
25. 3.1825	Stone, messuage & farm	John White (yeoman)	£35	48/14/51/12
25. 3.1825	Bonehill, Hamlyn's Northway, & Lower Barton	Thomas Hannaford (yeoman) & William Hannaford (yeoman)	£105	48/14/43/8

[b]y the late 18th century the two farms on the south side of the stream belonged to Lord Ashburton. They were amalgamated at some time in the early 19th century, and became Lower Bonehill.

The subsequent nine-year lease renewal in 1825 included Hamlyn's Northway and was granted to Thomas and William Hannaford, yeomen, by Lady Ashburton (Table 7).

The second Lord Ashburton married Anne Cunningham on 17th September, 1805 but died without issue on 15th February, 1823, aged only 40; Dymond (1876, p. 29) recalled that, on the second Lord Ashburton's death, his Widecombe estates (except for Bagtor), all still subject to the 99-year term created on John Wotton's death in 1746, passed to Miss Margaret Baring (his mother's niece, *i.e.*, the niece of the first Lady Ashburton, Elizabeth Baring). Leases on numerous Devon properties, including three in Widecombe-in-the-Moor, were then granted by Anne Selby (see Table 7). Lysons and Lysons (1822, p. 556) noted that Spitchwick was actually occupied by George Leach, Esq., in 1822.

According to Hemery (1983, p. 673), Widecombe Church Records for 1816 record a birth to Elias Hannaford, yeoman of Bunhill; presumably, Elias lived at Lower Bonehill Farm.

Name	Date of Indenture	Age at indenture	Occupation	Indentured until	Pay	Doc. folio number
	Table 8. – Thomas Hannaford's indentured workers at Lower Bonehill farmstead (data from Widecombe History Group, 2004)					
Mary Eascott*	16.10.1801	11	housewifery	21 or marriage	board & lodgings	305
Susanna Smerdon	3.10.1790	?	housewifery	21 or marriage	meat, drink, apparel, etc.	499
Jane Leaman: born 1811	7. 5.1827	16	housewifery	21 or marriage	board, lodgings	347
William Lee	7. 5.1827	16	husbandman	21	board, lodging, etc.	349
John Widdicombe	7. 5.1827	17	husbandman	21	board, lodgings	361
Mary Ruby	7. 5.1827	14	husbandman (sic.)	21	board, lodging, etc	362

Widecombe History Group (2004) recorded Thomas Hannaford as the employer of numerous indentured young people in 1801 and 1827 at Bunhill (undoubtedly Lower Bonehill) (Table 8).

William and Thomas Hannaford's 1825 lease (Table 7) was for nine years. In 1843, the farmstead was occupied (presumably as tenant under a new lease) by William Hannaford (farmer aged 40), his wife Nancy (35) and their seven children, Samuel Hannaford (agricultural labourer), and Harriet French (15) farm servant. The fields, which totalled 73.064 acres (29.56 ha), are listed in Table 9, which is based partially on Beeson & Masterman (1979, p.10, *et seq.*) and the hand-written notes about the 1841 Census on Widecombe Parish Chest copy). The 1843 field names are shown in Figure 41. Little change from arable to pasture occurred from 1843 to 1953 (see Table 9) but, for the past several decades, all land still farmed has been put to permanent pasture.

Today, four different units (Fig. 41 (1, 2, 3, & 4)) are collectively known as Honey but, in 1843, only the higher portion of the field (Fig. 41 (3, 4)) was called Honey; it seems that originally, only the small part of the field adjacent to Middle Bonehill's orchard (see Table 9 and Figs. 29 and 30) was Honey, suggesting it may have housed an apiary.

The 1845 Tithe Apportionment cited 72*a.* 1*r.* 28*p.* for Lower Bonehill and also showed that, in addition to this farmstead, Margaret Baring owned numerous other Widecombe area estates (*e.g.*, Higher and Lower Natsworthy, Great and Little Northway, part of North Hall, Coombe, part of Display, Scobitor, Spitchwick), none of which she occupied herself (Brown, 1997, p. 12). Actually, however, she only retained these estates until 1845, when the 99-year term of the trust established under Rev. John Wotton's 1746 Will expired.

It was shown in Chapter 3 that, under Rev. John Wotton's Will, subject to terms of the 99-year trust established after his death on 5th November, 1746, his Widecombe estates had been entailed to his brother Richard, then to his nephew Samuel Wotton, and then to

NB* in an unusual note, F. Wilkinson on 21.2.2001 stated "this was at Higher Bonehill" – the reason for this statement is unknown.

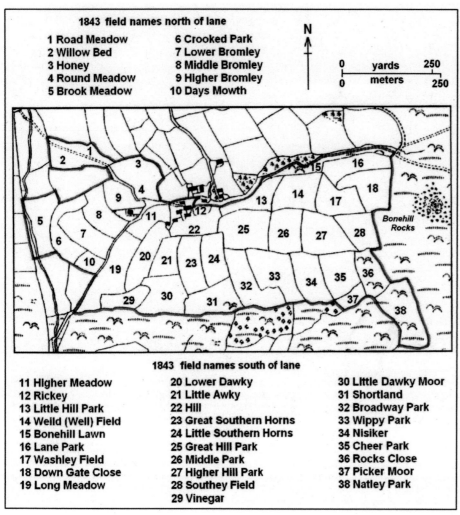

1843 field names north of lane

1 Road Meadow	6 Crooked Park
2 Willow Bed	7 Lower Bromley
3 Honey	8 Middle Bromley
4 Round Meadow	9 Higher Bromley
5 Brook Meadow	10 Days Mowth

1843 field names south of lane

11 Higher Meadow	20 Lower Dawky	30 Little Dawky Moor
12 Rickey	21 Little Awky	31 Shortland
13 Little Hill Park	22 Hill	32 Broadway Park
14 Weild (Well) Field	23 Great Southern Horns	33 Wippy Park
15 Bonehill Lawn	24 Little Southern Horns	34 Nisiker
16 Lane Park	25 Great Hill Park	35 Cheer Park
17 Washley Field	26 Middle Park	36 Rocks Close
18 Down Gate Close	27 Higher Hill Park	37 Picker Moor
19 Long Meadow	28 Southey Field	38 Natley Park
	29 Vinegar	

Figure 41. Lower Bonehill Farm field names in 1843 (see Table 9).

Samuel's male heirs; but Samuel had died unmarried and intestate on 2nd June, 1780. As a result, Anna Maria Wotton's heir claimed the estates.

Anna Maria had married Estcourt Cresswell, Esq. in 1771 and her only daughter, Anne Cresswell, married Rev. Thomas Fry in 1802, but died childless in December, 1811. Hence, both the direct and the fraternal Wotton lines had died out by 1845 (*i.e.*, by the end of the 99-year term). As a result, the estates reverted to be vested in the heirs of Estcourt Cresswell, under a settlement by his wife (the former Anna Maria Wotton – Rev. John Wotton's daughter - who had died on 30th September, 1772, aged 26, according to a monument inside St. Mary's Church, Bibury, Gloucestershire). Although contested by a Samuel Wotton, Thomas Fry won his claim to a life interest in the original John Wotton's (of Englebourne) estates (including Widecombe, Spitchwick and Blagdon Manors – and thus, including Lower Bonehill Farm). Rev. Fry became Lord of Widecombe Town Manor until his death on 27th March, 1860.

According to White's (1850, p. 451) compendium, "Blackslade belongs to Mr. W. Norrish and Lord Cranstoun, Sir W. P. Carew, Mr. Bastard, and many small free-holders have estates in the Parish" of Widecombe; White reported there were 1,106 inhabitants in Widecombe Parish in 1850, which comprised 10,614 acres and 4,700 open-common acres. The Lord of Widecombe Town Manor, Rev. Thomas Fry, was amongst the guests who attended the 1850 Widecombe Fair (Widecombe and District History Group, 2007, p. 2); it seems likely he had no actual residence within the Parish. The 1851 Census did not record anyone living at Lower Bonehill (unless possibly the Andrew West family from North Bovey lived there, *i.e.*, Andrew West 35, lodger and head of family, agricultural labourer, Agnes (32, wife), and Elizabeth (6, born North Bovey).

Table 9. – Lower Bonehill Farm fields – 1843 to 1953

(bold type - those still part of Lower Bonehill in 1999; italicised - those retained only in part)

O.S. field number	Field name in 1949	Probable field name in 1843	1953 acres	1843 use	1953 use	1906 O.S. map number	Tithe map number
5145	**House, Yard etc**	House, Yard, etc.	0.906	-	homestead	748 part	269
5545	Rickey	Rickey	0.236	pasture	arable	747	270
5441	*Waste*	Hill	1.649	-	waste	746	271
8756 part	**Waste**	Bonehill Lawn	1.367	R (?)	waste	728 part	272
9555	**Lane Park**	Lane Park	1.830	arable	arable	730	273
9949	**Down Gate Field**	Down Gate Close	2.333	arable	arable	731	274
9047	**Dashley Field**	Washley Field	2.068	arable	arable	736	275
9639	**Southey Field**	Southey Field	1.890	arable	arable	735	276
8738	Higher Hill Park	Higher Hill Park	2.793	arable	arable	737	277
9728	Rocks Park	Rocks Close	1.659	pasture	brake	734	278
9128	Chair Park	Cheer Park	2.243	arable	arable	738	279
9322	Picker	Picker Moor	0.641	pasture	rough run	789	279(a)
8327	Nisiker	Nisiker	2.262	arable	arable	739	280
8049	Well Field	Weild Field	2.283	arable	arable	727	281
7739	Middle Hill Park	Middle Park	2.273	arable	arable	741	282
6947	Little Hill Park	Little Hill Park	1.598	arable	arable	742	283
6640	Great Hill Park	Great Hill Park	3.047	arable	arable	743	284
7428	Diphay Park	Wippy Park (4)	2.893	arable	arable	740	285
6626	Broadway Park	Broadway Park	2.749	arable	pasture	786	286
5832	Little Southern Horn	Little Southern Horns	1.823	arable	pasture	744	287
5823	Shortland	Shortland	2.214	arable	pasture	784 & 785	288
5231	Great Southern Horn	Great Southern Horns	2.072	arable	arable	745	289
4633	Little Awky	Little Awky	1.378	arable	pasture	749	290
5145 part	**Buildings & Mowey**	Buildings & Mowey	above	meadow	homestead	748 part	291
4134	*Lower Dawky*	Lower Dawky	2.154	meadow	meadow	750	292
4234	**Higher Dawky Mead**	Higher Meadow	1.258	meadow	meadow	751	293
3230	Long Meadow	Long Meadow	3.130	meadow	meadow	756	294
4524	Little Dawky Moor	Lower Dawky Moor	2.460	pasture	moor	783	295
3523	Vinegar	Vinegar	1.156	arable	arable	781	296
3954/4149	**Honey**	Honey	2.265}	meadow	meadow	711}	306
3954/4149	**Honey**	Round Meadow	}	meadow	meadow	711}	307
2459 }	**Road Meadow**	Road Meadow	2.405}	meadow	meadow	707}	323
2459 }	**Road Meadow**	Willow Bed	}	pasture	meadow	707}	324
1443	Brook Meadow	Brook Meadow	2.418	pasture	meadow	760	327
1840	Crooked Park	Crooked Park	1.974	pasture	arable	759	328
3648	Bonehill House land	Higher Bromley	1.700	arable	Bonehill Hse	753 & 754	329
2944	Bonehill House land	Middle Bromley	2.040	arable	Bonehill Hse	755	330
2539	Lower Brimhay	Lower Bromley	2.166	arable	arable	758	331
2632	Days' Mowth	Days Mowth	0.695	meadow	pasture	757	332 (or 322)
0617	Natty Park	Natley Park	3.036	arable	brake	791	402

N.B.: In the 21st century, several official field numbers printed on O.S. maps were replaced and recorded by the Department for Environment, Food, and Rural Affairs (Defra) when it implemented the English Single Payment Scheme.

Dymond (1876, p. 31) recalled that:

> The Chancery proceedings, which had set in after the death of the Rev. John Wotton, had now become a tangled Maze which no lay pen could describe, nor legal subtlety unravel. At least ten suits in Chancery were being prosecuted at the same time, when the Gordian knot was finally cut by a decree of the Court under which, in September, 1867, the extensive and scattered estates, so carefully tied up by the will of Rev. John Wotton in 1746, and which had now been the subject of litigation for more than a century were sold in lots by auction to various purchasers

The court case Coope v. Cresswell was crucial for the Widecombe properties. As early as 3rd June, 1867, C. H. Mallock was advised that, because the Creswell Manors in Widecombe were soon to be sold, it would be prudent to have the boundaries of his Dunstone Manor defined by setting up a few boundarystones (DRO 48/13/4/7/16). In a Decree of the High Court of Chancery, the judge, Vice-Chancellor Malins, directed Mr. Pantin (auctioneer of Malmesbury, Wiltshire) to sell the contested properties. The Chief Clerk and the Plaintiff's Solicitors issued a notice of the auction sale of freehold properties extending to 1,300 acres in the parishes of Widecombe-in-the-Moor, Holne, and Staverton, and the borough of Ashburton, on 9th August 1867. Messrs. Buckland and Rendell of Newton Abbot were noted as the auctioneers and estate agents from whom, amongst many others countrywide, particulars could be obtained. This notice, as published in *Trewman's Exeter Flying Post* on 25th September, 1867, stated the auction would be at the Globe Hotel, Newton Abbot, on Thursday 26th September, 1867, at three o'clock, the property to be offered as 21 lots. Included, using their spelling, were the residential manor and estate of Spitchweek (Lot 1), the manor and estates of "Blackdown" (called "'Blackaton," otherwise "Blagdon Pipard"' in the advertisement's preamble) (Lot 7), "Higher and Lower Natsworthy" (Lot 8), "Stone" (Lot 9), "Coombe" (Lot 10), "Bonehill" (Lot 11 - 72a. 1r. 28p., with right of common over the Widecombe Town Manor of 706 acres), "Great and Little Northway" (Lot 12), "Scobitor" (Lot 13), the Manor of Widdecombe in the Moor, otherwise Widdecombe Town, (Lot 14 - extending over 706 acres and a tract of 44a. 1r. 11p. of 'Meadow, Arable, and Moor Land, known as "Bartons" and "North Hall"'), and "The Old Sun" in Widdecombe village (Lot 15).

At the auction, the Manor of Widecombe-in-the-Moor and North Hall were apparently bought by Mrs. Caroline Mason Drake (neé Brodrick) who had married Mr. Thomas Edward Drake jun. Esq., county solicitor, Exeter, on 22nd May 1855. Worthy (1874) wrote that:

> About five years since the whole of the property was sold, and Mrs. Drake (niece of the late Vicar of Widecombe, the Rev. J. H. Mason), became the purchaser of the Manor of Widecombe.

Blagdon Pipard (Blackdown) was bought by Isaac Lang, but who bought Bonehill (clearly Lower Bonehill) has not yet been traced. Middle Bonehill Farm was outside the web of the Chancery proceedings; as already noted, that freehold property was bought at a later auction in 1869 by Wm. K. Kennaway, after having been owned and occupied by the Smerdon family for several generations. It is difficult to surmise what affect the dramatic changes in absentee ownership had on the lives of the tenants and families of Lower Bonehill and so many other Widecombe farmsteads; indeed, how aware were the local farmers of the turmoil and confusion about ownership of the land on which they lived?

Who occupied Lower Bonehill (Table 6) during the early 19th century is unclear currently and it is unknown when the several present-day barns at Lower Bonehill ceased to be occupied as homes. Kelly (1873, pp. 424-5) and Dymond (1875, p. 8) cited Richard Rowe, farmer, living at Bunhill; this was probably Lower Bonehill because George Hannaford and Richard Waldron occupied Middle and Higher Bonehill, respectively. In 1890, Peter Hannaford occupied a house and land of 42*a*. 2*r*. 2*p*. (= 42.5125 acres) at Bunhill owned by Andrew Windeat - apparently Lower Bonehill (Widecombe Poor Rate Register 1890, entry 29). Other Bunhill residents (not currently associated with specific properties) were farmer Joseph Willcocks (Kelly, 1893, pp. 669-70) and William Harvey (Kelly, 1902, pp. 359-60)*.

Kelly (1873) recorded Edwin Smerdon living at Bunhill Villa, which included 3.74 acres (fields 329 & 330, known as Higher & Middle Bromley) formerly part of the Lower Bonehill Farm. The 1881 Census recorded Edwin Smerdon (farmer of 75 acres), his brother Richard, Mrs. Ann Leaman (general servant, 64, widow), and William Leaman "farm servant (in door)" (14), all in the Bunhill Villa household. The 1890 Widecombe Poor Rate Register showed Edwin Smerdon owned just over 72.5 acres in Bunhill, but that he occupied only 12½ acres while Richard Willcocks occupied the remaining 60 acres. (To add confusion, the 1890 Register recorded over 200.5 acres in what it called Bunhill, although Beeson & Masterman's (1979) data suggested the 1841 Tithe record reflects only a little over 157.2 acres.)

In the early 20th century, Lower Bonehill Farm was back close to its earlier size. By at least 1910, Frank Nosworthy was the tenant (Kelly, 1910, p. 805); he retained tenancy until 1972. Rendell & Sawdye offered the freehold of Lower Bonehill Farm at auction at the Golden Lion, Ashburton, on 18th June, 1919; despite a large attendance, slow bidding started at £1,500 and the property was withdrawn at £1,800. Alexander Nelson Radcliffe, who had bought Bagpark Estate in April 1909, then acquired the greater part (66.9 acres) of Lower Bonehill Farm (Conveyance on Sale dated 25th March, 1920). A new tenancy agreement for "Bonehill Farm" (71*a*. 1*r*. 2*p*.) was drawn up with Frank Nosworthy of "Bonehill" at a yearly rent of £98; this agreement dated 30th October, 1920, stipulated:

---

*A Peter Hannaford, not a unique name by any means, occupied a house and land of just over 66 acres on Blackslade Estate (owned by Mrs. Dymond) in 1890 (Widecombe Poor Rate Register); it is possible that he also worked Lower Bonehill; a Peter Hannaford (47 of Widecombe) dwelt at Tunhill Farm and farmed 50 acres in 1881 (1881 Census) with his wife Elizabeth (49 of Buckland), son John H. (22), and five daughters (Mary E. 19, Louisa J. 17, Laura E. 13, Sarah A. 11 and Florence E. 8).

and interest at the same Rate [£6 per cent.] on the Amount to be expended by the Landlord in replacing the existing thatch Roofs with Slate. such Interest to become payable as additional Rent from Ladyday 1921.

At that time, more than 35 acres (over 49%) were said to be in arable (as was also the case in 1949).

Radcliffe acquired the remainder of the former Lower Bonehill Farm land, Brook Meadows (field 327, old O.S. 760, new O.S. 1443, 2.42 acres; see Fig. 41), by conveyance on 8th May, 1931, from the Trustees of a Marriage Settlement (dated 18th November, 1892), who had acquired the field on 9th May, 1924 (but it is unknown from whom). This field had been included in the 1841 Tithe listing for Lower Bonehill. After the house at Lower Bonehill was condemned for human habitation, Bonehill Bungalow (Fig. 35(BB)) was built just to the east in 1935 for the tenant. Eventually, part of Lower Bonehill farmhouse's slated roof fell in. By 1949, Frank Nosworthy* held a yearly Lady Day Tenancy at an apportioned annual rent of £86; when the lease was surrendered on 29th September. 1972, the rent was £125 per year.

By 1930, Radcliffe had become Lord of Widecombe Town Manor. The tenanted Lower and Middle Bonehill farms were included when Bagpark Estate was put to auction by Radcliffe's executors in October 1949. Lower Bonehill (Lot 7) 69a.1r.12p. (69.325 acres) was withdrawn unsold but was purchased afterwards by Francis Hamlyn on 17th February, 1950, as attested by the Conveyance from Right Hon. Ronald Gorell (Baron Gorell of Brampton), Arthur Bowen von Straubenzec, and Percy Robert Wace to William George Reed and Francis Hamlyn. After Francis Hamlyn died three years later, on 23rd June, 1953, Lower Bonehill Farm (still with Frank Nosworthy as tenant) was bought for £2,000 on 26th October, 1953 from Marianne Margaret Hamlyn (of Dunston Court, spinster), Harold Gaye Michelmore, and Jeffry Michelmore (solicitors) by Jasper Thomas French, retired farmer, who himself died on 21st November, 1971.

On 23rd May, 1972, an application was filed under the Town and Country Planning Act 1971 with Newton Abbot Rural District Council by the Executors of Jasper French to restore Lower Bonehill Farmhouse for human occupation; conditional planning permission was granted on 16th August, 1972. Frank Nosworthy's long tenancy terminated on 29th September, 1972. Almost immediately, either as executors or as Jasper French's heirs, Linda Tremaine Nosworthy and Phyllis Thirza French of Inglemoor, Widecombe, sold the farmstead in three parts, *viz*:

(a) some 54 acres to William Wallace Whitley of Holwell on 17th October, 1972, for £23,250; this included the tenant's bungalow (Bonehill Bungalow – Fig. 35(BB)) built in 1935, which was sold on to Mrs. Joan Perkins (who lived there with her family until her death),

* Many referred to him as Uncle Frank, not to be confused with Big Frank and his son Little Frank; little Frank, who married Isobel Daw, died in 1976 but not before winning the Widecombe Fair's annual Uncle Tom Cobley Novelty Race in 1931, 1932, 1933, and 1934 and, on his death, his family donated the Frank Nosworthy Memorial Cup for the first local runner home in the ongoing Uncle Tom Cobley race (Widecombe and District History Group, 2007, pp. 93-4).

(**b**) four fields comprising 9.49 acres below Bonehill Rocks and south of Bonehill Lane) to William Wallace Whitley (purchaser) and George Barnes Pearson (of Ipswich) and Algernon Patrick Frances Rothman (of Winchester) (sub-purchasers) on 19th October, 1972, for £3,075, and

(**c**) the house, barns, and some adjacent fields totalling 7.51 acres to William Wallace Whitley (purchaser), and Malcolm and Joyce Margaret Phyllis Scott of Basingstoke (sub-purchasers) for £14,925 on 19th October, 1972.

Proposed new elevations for the farmhouse, and a new granite bridge just to the west across the stream, were drawn by G. J. Wood (architect of Andover, Hampshire); plans followed in March 1974 for two stairways (at the east and west ends of the house), windows, and plumbing. Although Malcolm Scott died on 14th October, 1974, two years after purchasing the house, further internal drawings were prepared by G. J. Wood in January and March, 1975. However, on 22nd March, 1976, John Sydney Charles Smith and Georgina Ann Smith of Park Farm, Bourn, Cambridgeshire bought part (**c**) for £20,000 and (in a separate contract) part (**b**) for £2,500. It is uncertain precisely when renovations were carried out; they do not match Wood's plans in numerous respects. As mentioned previously, Tom Nosworthy moved the granite slabs from the farmhouse byre floor to the barn to the southwest (Fig. 35(2)) before April 1974; he was also called in to help the contractors cope with slating the main roof. The late Percy Bishop (of Bonehill Bungalow) recalled that, when the contractors were inserting new oak ceiling beams through the granite walls, they cut one about a foot too short, so he 'took care of' the unusable wood for them. John Smith had J. Roberts (Contractor) plan a land-drainage scheme for a 300mm pipe (with inlet chamber) for the stream to be taken 40m underground southwest of the house, and also for a network of land drains in the fields (called Honey), across the road to the northwest; these plans were filed with the Exeter Divisional Office of the Ministry of Agricultural, Fisheries, and Food on 27th November, 1979, and the work was soon completed.

Anthony Victor Smith and Betty Kathleen Smith purchased Lower Bonehill Farm for £80,000 on 20th June, 1980; this included parts (**b**) and (**c**). The *Teignmouth Post* (5th July, 1985) noted Lower Bonehill Farm (*ca.* 17 acres) being offered for sale by Bettesworth (Estate Agents) at an asking price of £150,000; the property was bought by Neil and Leila Esther Godfrey of Barnes, London, in March 1986. In June 1990, it was bought by the current owners.

Higher Bonehill Farm

North of Bonehill Lane stands the thatched, granite and mortar built, Higher Bonehill farmhouse (Fig. 42). The porch at the lower end suggests that the house was probably built after the longhouse period. The farm property changed little between the 1843 Tithe Map, when

Figure 42. Higher Bonehill Farmstead viewed looking west from Thornhill Lane.

the fields totalled 35.769 acres (10.428 ha), and its sale at auction in Newton Abbot on behalf of the owner and occupier, Mrs. B. M. Cole, on 26th March, 2003. Table 10 and Figure 29 show that a large proportion of the fields was used for arable in 1843 but, towards the end of the 20th century, all fields were permanent rough grazing; although some of the dryer land had been dug over for potatoes during the 1939 World War - see below. The June 1977 Ministry of Agriculture returns showed no farms in the immediate area were listed as cropping holdings (Beeson and Masterman, 1979, p. *viii*). Figure 43 shows the field names used in 1843 (mainly as collated by Beeston and Masterman, 1979). Today, Down Gate Field and Higher Bunny abound with rabbits – probably Bunny in these names refers to rabbits, although these fields were to arable when the Tithe Map was made.

Elias Cuming, apparently living at Higher Bonehill, employed George Leaman as a husbandman (until he was 21 years of age) under indenture dated 12th October, 1795 (Widecombe History Group, 2004, folio 459); this was probably the Elias Cuming, yeoman, listed for 1783 (only) amongst Devon freeholders (Friends Devon Archives, 2007). The 1841 Census recorded John White aged 60 (farmer) as occupier, along with Thomas Webber (independent), John Hext 15 (apprentice), and Susan Warren 25 (farm servant). In the 1851 Census, only John White (unmarried, retired farmer, age 70, born in Widecombe) and Thomas Webber (lodger, unmarried, former agricultural labourer, age 79, born in Manaton) were listed. Both census reports showed Elias Cumming owned Higher Bonehill; he also owned, but did not occupy, Pittonspark (59*a*. 1*r*. 31*p*.) and Stotits Tenement (10*a*. 2*r*. 6*p*.) (1845 Tithe Apportionment, Brown, 1997, p. 12). Elias Cuming and Elias Cumming are probably either same person, or father and son. Kelly (1873, 1883) and White (1878/9, p. 849) merely recorded Richard Waldron living in Bunhill, but the 1881 Census listed Richard Waldron (carpenter, 56, from Lidford) living at Higher Bonehill with his wife Hannah (48, from North Bovey), and their four children born in Widecombe, namely William N. (16), Mary M. (10), Ellen G. (7), and Albert R. (6). Kelly (1889, p. 613) referred only to Mrs. Anna Waldron, farmer. According to the 1890 Widecombe Poor Rate Register, Higher Bonehill farmhouse and land, extending to 36 acres, 0 rods, and 5 perches (*i.e.*, 36.031 acres = 14.581 hectares) owned by E. J. Cumming and occupied by Elias Cumming.

James Beard lived at Higher Bonehill from at least 1923 (Kelly, 1923, p. 805; 1926, p. 846; 1930), being listed as farmer in 1930; a photo of him sowing seed in 1931 by Beatrice Chase

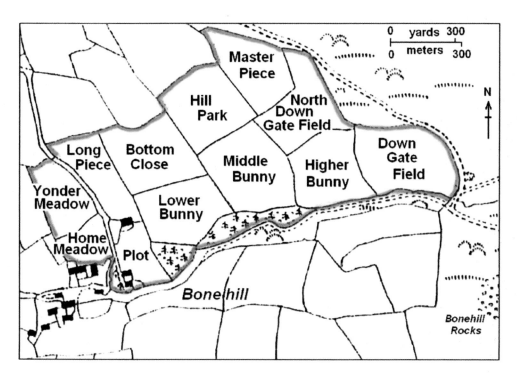

Figure 43. Higher Bonehill Farm field names in 1843; the farmhouse and barn are in Plot; the building at the southern end of Long Piece is a derelict barn. The Farm's four separated fields (to the west) are shown in Figure 30.

was reproduced by Woods (2000, p. 20). He was Anthony Beard's great uncle, who helped support his several children by working as postman in addition to farming (*pers. commn*, A. E. Beard, 1998). In fact, he must have been living there several years earlier because, Herbert Henry Hannaford's diary for September 1909 recorded 'Young Beard for Bunhill' being present on 25th September, 1909, at the Widecombe Town Manor Beating of the Bounds (see Brewer, 2002, p. 82, with photocopy of the diary page). Woods (1996, p. 105) recorded that James Beard, born in 1861, became an auxiliary postman in 1872 when only 11 years old, although the Post Office normally did not hire boys under 14; he retired from the Post Office in 1931 after 59 years service and died in 1942, being buried in Widecombe church-yard. These details align with Hemery's (1983, p.655) note that

> In the days of pedestrian and pony-back postmen, a path called 'Postman's Path' was in use between Widecombe and Bonehill; a clapper bridge carrying it across the streamlet falling from Bonehill Rocks was damaged by American troops during the last war and afterwards painstak-ingly rebuilt by Mrs Cole's former husband, Bert Dunn.

The location of this bridge was not specified by Hemery, but it was probably the small bridge across the East Webburn River in the field originally called Marsh (O.S field 1263, old number 704), that Betsy Cole used to call one of her 'Wooder Fields'. However, the East

Table 10. Higher Bonehill Farm Fields (1843-1950)

O.S. field number	Field name	Acres O.S. map	Acres 1950 deed	1843 use	1950 use	old O.S. field number	Tithe map number
7877	Master Piece	2.06	2.069	-	arable	665	251
8577 & 8671	North Down Gate Field	2.30	2.298	arable	arable	664	252
8863	Higher Bunny	2.28	2.265	arable	arable	729	253 & 254
9964	Down Gate Field	2.85	2.855	fir (?)	arable & moor	732	255
7957	Plantation	0.91	0.933	arable	wood	726	256
7863	Middle Bunny	2.77	2.756	arable	arable	725	257
7272	Hill Park	2.45	2.466	pasture	arable	666	258
6465	Bottom Close	2.48	2.464	pasture	arable	724	260
6857	Lower Bunny	2.22	2.187	-	pasture	723	261
6351 }	Plantation	1.60 }	0.521	-	wood	722	262
6351 }	Plot	1.60 }	1.108	pasture	paddock	721	263
5948	House, Barn, Garden	0.319	0.319	pasture	house, buildings	720	264 & 265
5554	Home Meadow	0.86	0.879	meadow	pasture	716	297
5762	Long Piece	1.71	1.699	pasture	pasture	719	298
4967	Road		0.350	road	lane	718	298 (a)
5160	Yonder Meadow	1.49	1.507	meadow	pasture	717	299 (or 229)
2168	*Winter Lears*	3.15	3.138	pasture	pasture	708	319
1777	*Little Winter Lears*	2.07	2.077	pasture	pasture	679	320
1263	*Marsh*	2.98	2.973	pasture	pasture	704	322
1352	*Marsh Meadow*	1.27	1.284	pasture	pasture	705	326
	TOTAL	35.769+road	36.148				

N.B.: Because Tithe-map fields 319, 320, 322, and 326 were not part of the farm after 2003, their names are italicised.

Webburn is wholly different from the small stream that rises in the mire just north of Bonehill Rocks and flows through Bonehill hamlet, where a council maintained bridge now spans the stream.

Kelly (1933, p. 821; 1935) recorded Edwd. Dunn living at Higher Bonehill; he had been Uncle Tom Cobley at Widecombe Fair from 1928 until his death early in 1938, when one of his sons (Robert Dunn) briefly took over as Uncle Tom (Widecombe and District Local History Group, 2007, p. 86). Kelly (1939, pp. 840-1) listed Albt. Dunn as the occupier. His wife, Betsy Muriel Dunn (born 4 September, 1911, daughter of Ernest Albert Tarr) was remembered until recently by occasional elderly walkers who recalled enjoying her farm-fare during the lean World War II years. She herself recalled (*pers. cmmn*, Betsy Cole, 1997) digging potatoes in the fields below Bonehill Rocks during the War, and her late (first) husband, Albert Dunn, repairing damage caused by war training to the small bridge across the East Webburn River leading to Wooder (probably the bridge referred to by Hemery, 1983, p. 655). Mr. and Mrs. Dunn purchased the farm (simply called Bonhill or Bonehill

Farm in the deed) on 1st November, 1950, for £2,250 from Daphne Florence Anna Russell (of The Vicarage, Amport, near Andover, Hampshire, wife of Alban Edward Russell). The property's deeds record that on 25th October, 1950, an official solicitor's search recorded 'no subsisting entries' had been found and that it was unknown for how long Mrs. Russell had owned the farm. At the time of purchase, Mrs. Russell afforded the Dunn's a £2,000 mortgage at 4% interest; the outstanding mortgage balance (£1,800) was discharged to Mrs. Russell (who then lived at Moorcroft, Cassington, Oxford) by Betsy Cole (widow Dunn) in 1994. Albert Dunn had committed suicide on 3rd October, 1959 and, 16 years later, on 1st November, 1975, Betsy Dunn married Harold Augustus Cole (then 68, of 26 Market Street, Buckfastleigh) in Widecombe Church (Rev. William E. Brown officiating). The Coles installed a small pump to bring water to the house when electricity was first connected to the property in the 1990s; until then, all water used in the house had to be carried from the leat to the north of the house - a chilling task in winter. Harold died in hospital in about 2000. Betsy Cole, by then also permanently hospitalised, sold the farmstead at auction in Newton Abbot as two lots on 26th March, 2003; the bidding was very keen. The final bid price was £380,000 for all the farmstead (26.65 acres = 10.79 ha) except the 'Wooder fields' (O.S. fields 1263, 1352, 1777, 2168, totalling 9.47 acres or 3.84 ha) which were bought as the second lot by a local farmer for £31,000. The thatched farmhouse roof had fallen in a year or so before the auction. The new owner had the roof of the house and the large barn to the south re-thatched, and sank a borehole for water; the building interiors have been extensively refurbished.

Other Bonehill hamlet residences

Farther down Bonehill lane, on the north side, lies the more modern house which Kelly (1873, 1893) listed as "Bonhill Villa" occupied by Edwin Smerdon (Fig. 35(BV(BH))). This property is called Bunhill Cottage on the 1904 revision of the 1889 O.S. 6 inch to the mile map; it occupies the field called Higher Bromley which, in 1843, was an arable field and part of Lower Bonehill Farm. When Robert Vicary lived there during World War I, Kelly (1910, p. 805; 1914, p. 831; 1919, p. 778) recorded it merely as "Bunhill". Later, the property was owned by Mr. and Mrs. Denis Hanley, who ran a substantial poultry business from the buildings immediately north of the house. The property was sold to the Palmes but, following Mr. and Mrs. Robin Palmes' separation, it was divided into two separate permanent houses in 1997. The main house is now Bonehill House. The former coach-house to the north, which had been used for studio classes by Mrs. Shan Palmes for some years, was renovated as her permanent residence named Bonehill Cottage (Fig. 35(BC)). This cottage was purchased by the present occupiers in 2006. Bonehill House itself was sold in 1997; it has been resold and remodelled a couple of times since, and was being advertised for sale late in 2008.

The compact Bonehill Bungalow (Fig. 35(BB)) originally built for Frank Nosworthy in 1935, was bought by Joan Perkins in 1972 (see above). She lived there for many years with her husband before her death a few years ago; the property continues in the family. Percy Bishop also lived at this bungalow for many years before his death.

Hence, there are now six homes in the ancient Bunhill hamlet - three old and three modern. Many families and much hard work lie hidden in the mists of past ages. Much has remained unchanged, but a significant amount has changed and continues to change, ever more rapidly. Many of the changes were predictable in view of the changes in society as a whole, but many other events were wholly unpredictable by anyone (*e.g.*, the early deaths of Cholmeley D'Oyly and of Rev. John Wotton) and had profound effects on the evolution of Bonehill and the whole Parish of Widecombe-in-the-Moor.

St Pancras Church at the heart of Widecombe in the Moor, from Thornton Lane above Bonehill, March 2009.

5

19TH CENTURY WIDECOMBE AND THE MASON FAMILY

Socially, Widecombe-in-the-Moor must have been a very interesting community in the 19th century, seeing many dramatic changes. Amongst the Devon freeholders, in 1762 one gentleman (Robert Hodge) and 17 yeomen were recorded in Widecombe, but, by 1799, freeholders in the Parish had declined to eight (Friends Devon Archives, 2007). The mid-19th century holds particular intrigue, coloured by the lives of Rev. James Holman Mason and his niece, Lady Caroline Drake.

Holman Mason, lieutenant in the Navy, was an Okehampton freeholder in 1783 (Friends Devon Archives, 2007). It is uncertain whether this was the same person as the Holman and Catherine Mason of Okehampton who, about a decade earlier, had a son (James Holman Mason) and a daughter (Sarah Hooper Mason), both of whom have frequently been referred to as illegitimate offspring of the Prince Regent (*e.g.*, Thomas, 1992) who became King George IV in 1820. Rev. S. Baring-Gould (1900*, p. 182), for example, wrote that this Sarah "...was believed to be of blood-royal with a bar sinister". While obviously subscribing to this belief whole-heartedly, and noting that both James and Sarah were both brought up at Court, Baring-Gould (1900, p. 189) concluded several pages (including considerable circumstantial evidence) by noting the mystery "... was never solved, and it is possible enough that the supposed paternity was due to idle gossip." Stemming from genealogical searches for his own forebears in the Plymouth Library, the Hartly Family History Centre, and the Okehampton Dartmoor Life Museum, Peter G. T. B. Harvey (1993, p. 4) determined that Sarah Hooper Mason was baptised on 24th March, 1774, and married James Brodrick on 28th November, 1805, in Okehampton; the couples' only child, Caroline Mason Brodrick, was born in 1806. Sarah was about five years younger than her brother, James Holman, who became a cleric.

Although actual plans for a new church at Two Bridges were reviewed in 1797 at Prince Hall (then Mr. Tyrwhitt's private house, now a hotel), the church was never built. For a while, church services were conducted at Prince Hall, which lies about 2 miles (3.2 km) east of present-day Princetown, an area Thomas Tyrwhitt was enthusiastic to develop. Tyrwhitt was Secretary to the Prince of Wales until he was elected MP for Okehampton in 1796 (until 1802). In 1805, Mr. (after 1812, Sir) Thomas Tyrwhitt was appointed Lord Warden of the

*The quotations from Baring-Gould (1900) are from the third edition of 1916; although a first edition has not been seen, there is no indication the third edition was more than a reprint of the first.

Stanneries. He was also responsible for founding Princetown, "so named after his friend the Prince Regent" who was Lord of the Manor, Prince of Wales, and Duke of Cornwall. Tyrwhitt had made plans to build a prison of war, including a chapel, on his own land in Princtown. He laid the foundation stone in March 1806 and that same year was elected MP for Plymouth.

On the 3rd February, 1808, the Duchy leased land two miles northeast of Princetown, adjacent to the new east-west turnpike road across Dartmoor, to Rev. James Holman Mason, where he built a cottage (Hemery, 1983, p. 433). It is unclear what use was made of the property initially; Hemery (1983, p. 457) asserted that:

> In 1839, when Rev. J. H. Mason occupied his new cottage – he called it 'Crockern Cottage', but the name 'Parson's' Cottage soon replaced it -

although he did not state explicitly that the cottage was first occupied in 1839. The site of Parson's Cottage is still named on modern Ordnance Survey maps.

Mason was appointed as the minister at the Dartmoor Church on 13th April, 1813, at the salary of £300 per annum, by the Admiralty Board which, through the Transport Office, was responsible for building the Princetown prison of war; at this time, Mason must have been a little over 40 years old. Rev. Mason was widely reported to have been chaplain to the Prince Regent. On 2nd January, 1814, following the first service ever conducted at the partially completed Princetown Church, Mason baptised two children, including his niece Caroline Brodrick, then aged about seven and described in the Baptismal Register as the daughter of a Plymouth merchant (Stanbrook, 1996, who stated the name was Broderick in the Baptismal Register). Princetown Church was apparently only completed late in 1814 or early 1815, just before the Battle of Waterloo, the end of the war, and the consequent repatriation of the French and American prisoners of war; in consequence, the buildings are said to have stood empty from 1816 until 1850 (Baring-Gould, 1899, p. 199; Stanbrook, 1996).

James Holman Mason was presented as Vicar of Widecombe-in-the-Moor on 3rd July, 1815 (Dymond, 1876, p. 21). According to Baring-Gould (1900, p. 182), Rev. Mason,

> when given the living of Widdecombe - to get him out of sight and mind - brought with him a large consignment of excellent port, and that drew to his parsonage such rare men as would brave the moors and storms for the sake of a carouse.

White (1850, pp.453-4) listed Rev. Jas. H. Mason, M.A., as current vicar of Widecombe and Treneglos, and chaplain of Tor Royal Chapel; it was noted that, as incumbent in Widecombe, Mason had 86a. 1r. 6p. (34.92 ha) of glebe and a good residence, the vicarage having been valued at £332 in 1831. He appears to have been Deputy Warden of Stanneries in 1852 [DRO QS/78/1/8]. James Mason clearly had close connections with the Duchy because in October 1916 (Crossing, 1901, p. 55) he was appointed to the official positions of Deputy Rider (Reeve) and Master Forester, posts which he retained until his death in 1860; the duties included authorising the official cattle and pony drifts on the Moor (*e.g.*, Hemery, 1983, p. 433).

Baring-Gould (1900, p. 182) referred to the young Caroline Brodrick's father (James Brodrick) as captain, presumably a merchant-ship's captain. According to Tim Wright (*pers. commn*, 2008), Sarah and James Brodrick separated in 1819 and the latter seems to have disappeared from the Dartmoor scene. Harvey (1993) discovered that this James had two further wives before dying in Charles Parish, Plymouth, on 25th March, 1843, in his seventies. Baring-Gould (1900, p.183) asserted Caroline's mother, Sarah, lived in a desolate cottage under Crockern Tor, and there languished and died, leaving her only daughter (Caroline) to the charge of her uncle, Rev. J. H. Mason; Baring-Gould seems not to have been aware that the 'desolate cottage' belonged to Mason. However, Harvey (1993) claimed that mother and daughter moved into Widecombe Vicarage, which does not seem unlikely.

Baring-Gould (1900, pp. 183-5) wrote that Caroline was sent to:

a famous school in Queen's Square, London, where she associated with girls belonging to families of the first rank ... her imperious manner commanded respect ...

The vicarage was by no means a good place in which a young girl should grow to maturity. The house was not frequented by men of the best character, and the wildest stories are told of the goings-on there in the forties and fifties.

Caroline was, however, a girl of exceptionally strong character; she was early called upon to hold her own with the associates of her uncle and frequenters of the vicarage, ...

Unhappily, she had been reared without any religious principles; her law was consequently her own caprice, fortunately held in check by a strong sense of personal dignity... she possessed furious passions, ...

A gentlemen named Darke [*sic*], visiting her uncle on some business, married Caroline, and soon after her uncle died suddenly, having made a will in her favour.

The vicarage was well furnished and contained articles of great value, in pictures, plate, etc., supposed to have been presented to him [presumably to James Holman Mason], but most likely obtained with money lent at Court to those temporarily embarrassed.

The manor had been sold, and was purchased by Mrs. Darke's [*sic*] trustees at her request, and from that time she insisted on being entitled "Lady" Darke [*sic*]; and into this she moved with her dogs, horses, and husband. ...

She ruled her husband, and indeed everyone with whom she came in contact. He cut off from social intercourse with his fellows ... [he] fell into degradation without making an effort to rise out of it.

Baring-Gould (1900, p. x) considered his book, although a "gossiping volume", a supplement to well-known works like Rowe's (1896) compendium *Perambulations of Dartmoor* and Crossing's (1888) *Amid Devonia's Alps*, and thus presumably to be a realistic reference source. His later novel, *Royal Georgie*, however, is a wholly fascinating parody of Caroline's life in and around Widecombe; thus, for example, (Baring-Gould, 1901, pp. 10-1):

The Reverend Josiah Thirkleby had been chaplain to the Prince of Wales till, in 1811, the latter had been appointed regent, whereupon the Reverend Josiah was dismissed to an incumbency far from town - in a word, to Wellcombe in the moor and out of the world. ...

Rennells (1999), without citing a source, mentioned that in 1845 Caroline Mason Drake (neé Brodrick), already the owner of Wooder and Coombe, purchased the lease of North Hall; if that date is correct, it must have been a lease for the residual term of the Wotton trust until 1867 (*i.e.*, the end of 99 years specified under Rev. Wotton's Will). Also, Caroline would have been Miss Brodrick in 1845, because it was not until the comparatively late age of about 49 that she married Thomas Edward Drake jun. Esq., son of T. E. Drake, Esq., County Solicitor of Exeter (a prominent Exeter family) on 22nd May, 1855. The wedding at Widecombe-in-the-Moor was performed by Rev. W. M. Paige, rector of Ilsington, according to an announcement in *Trewman's Exeter Flying Post* on 24th May, 1855 (*cf.*, Harvey, 1993, p. 4). Rev. Mason, Caroline's uncle, died suddenly in 1860. At some stage, Caroline certainly seems to have adopted the name Lady Drake. Although Baring-Gould wrote that she assumed this title on acquiring the manor after her marriage, one might conjecture that she might have taken the title when she bought the Lordship of the Manor of Widecombe and North Hall at the 1867 auction stipulated by the Court of Chancery. She was referred to incorrectly as Lady Darke (Harvey, p.4, who cited examples of both official documentary sources and Sylvia Sayer) by both Baring-Gould (1900) and Thomas (1992).

Hemery (1983, p. 673) considered the Rev. Mason's long incumbency from 1815 to 1860 to have been "part of the stable pattern of life on Dartmoor in those times." Woods (2000, p. 23) reproduced a portrait of the bald elderly Mr. Mason. Crossing, having been able to talk to people who still remembered Mason, wrote (Crossing, 1901, p. 55):

> Mr. Mason, who was chaplain to the Prince Regent and vicar of Treneglos and Warbstow, in Cornwall, was ... instituted to the vicarage of Widecombe, on the presentation of the Dean and Chapter of Exeter. In October of the following year Mr. Mason was appointed one of the deputy riders and master foresters of Dartmoor, on the decease of Mr. Edward Bray...
>
> From this time he began to take a strong interest in all matters pertaining to the Moor, acquainting himself with its topography, history, and traditions. He has been described as a cautious and practical antiquary, and though he himself made no contributions to Dartmoor literature, the results of his investigations are reflected in the writings of others, to whom he was always ready to impart information. His conclusions are certainly far more sound than those arrived at by some who have undertaken the examination of stone remains on the Moor.
>
> Mr. Mason was one of the old-fashioned school of parsons, and famous, among other things, for his hospitality and the excellence of his port. About 1842 a reading party from Oxford were staying at Brimpts, on Dartmoor, and during their visit attended Widecombe Church. Having been invited to dine with Mr. Mason, the conversation over their wine took a turn which called forth a remark by one of the party to the effect that he thought it a good thing the rotten boroughs were done away with. Mr. Mason instantly resented this. "What, sir," he said indignantly, "you tell me that! ---me, who was brought up by Sir Thomas Tyrwhitt, the confidential friend and favourite of George the Fourth, and who was member for___" Such views were dangerous in the eyes of this Moorland parson.
>
> Mr. Mason was the holder of about 600 acres of land in the Forest. He formed enclosures, and built a cottage, the ruins of which are still to be seen, close to the road below Crockern Tor.

He died at Widecombe in 1860, but was not laid to rest in the valley where he had dwelt so long. But he lies in the Dartmoor country, nevertheless, having been buried at Okehampton.

Crossing's (1901) measured statement contrasts with Baring-Gould's (1900) remarks cited above. Again, in a Chapter entitled "The Mysterious Lady Drake", Woods (2000, p. 23) quoted a hand-written article by Lady Sylvia Sayer, written in about 1950, which stated:

> the Reverend James Mason, occasionally dropped a hint or two over his excellent port as to his own and his sister's illustrious but illegitimate parentage. That sister, deserted by her husband, had died, leaving the little Caroline in James Mason's care – if care it could be called; for Parson Mason, exiled from Court to the wilds of Widecombe, was an embittered man who drank hard and kept strange company.

A folklore writer, Ray Thomas (1992), more recently added a very colourful picture of Lady Drake; it is unclear how much hard evidence exists for this newspaper article, which included (quoted from Harvey, 1993, p. 2):

> The real identity of Lady Darke (sic) is a mystery and her story begins in the early nineteenth century in Widecombe, where the vicar and his widowed sister with whom he lived were reputed to be the illegitimate offspring of the Prince Regent. They certainly lived well above their means. The sister had a daughter, Caroline, beautiful and expensively educated in London. She married someone called William Darke and later inherited her uncle's estate and retitled herself Lady Darke.
>
> She kept her husband firmly under her thumb and had a reputation for eccentricity. When a neighbour offended her, she spiked a doll and claimed it had the desired effect. Important visitors were collected in a carriage and pair resplendent in silver harness, but for normal errands the horses wore brass harness. Hubby, however, had to make do with a little trap used for collecting coal.
>
> She was a great socialiser and loved to play the piano for after dinner dances. When her cats had litters in the piano, the thing rusted, so she bought a barrel organ and hubby had to wind it in a corner. Unknown to her, he kept a bottle stashed there and one evening, when he got legless, he and the organ fell over, but, much to Caroline's delight, William broke the organ's fall and only he was damaged.
>
> William eventually died under the bed, having turned in there by mistake while drunk. Caroline considered a pig cloth adequate as a burial shroud and contemptuously consigned his body to 'his friends in Plymouth'.
>
> Her own demise allowed access to her secret room whose only key she kept in her garter. It was cobwebbed and knee deep in junk, with bank notes clogging some drawers and silver plate bearing crests from the court of the Prince Regent.
>
> Sadly, bundles of letters she had ordered to be destroyed on her death concealed forever the bloodline of the enigmatic Lady Darke.

Thomas subsequently conceded to Harvey (1993, p. 4) that his use of Darke (supposedly copied from reference books) instead of Drake, was mistaken.

Mrs. Thomas Drake was Lord of Widecombe Manor according to Morris (1870, pp. 887-8) and White (1878/9, p. 849). Lady Drake died suddenly on 14th March, 1885, at the Manor House, a widow without issue and intestate, her husband having died in 1883. A simple notice of death appeared on 18th March, 1885, in *Trewman's Exeter Flying Post* and, without mention of 'Lady', read merely:

> DRAKE – March 14, at the Manor House, Widdecombe-in-the-Moor, Caroline Mason, widow of Thomas E. Drake, jun. Esq.

Her trustees had to advertise for relatives, none apparently having visited her at Wooder Manor. All her assets seem to have been bequeathed to progeny of her father's third marriage (Harvey, 1993, p. 4), including:

a. Albert Brodrick, to whom Wooder Manor passed; he was listed as Lord of the Manor of Widecombe in Kelly's Directories for 1889 (p. 613), 1893, and 1897 (no one having been shown for 1883), and

b. Caroline Ann Brodrick: who was living in Charles Parish, Plymouth, when she married Samuel Harvey on 15th April, 1847, whom she outlived to die in Yelverton on 12th November, 1919.

These details are corroborated by the contemporary directories. Billings (1857, p. 546) noted William Smerdon as Wooder resident, but Thomas Drake was listed as occupier of Wooder Manor in Kelly Directories for 1866 (p. 1059) and 1883 (p. 500), while Albert Brodrick was so listed in the 1889 Kelly (p. 613).

However, while the association of the Prince Regent's name with Prince Hall and Princetown, the association of James Holman Mason with Princetown and the Duchy, and his incumbency of Widecombe-in-the-Moor, and many other details are well documented, there is a major problem about the bar-sinister issue associated with James Holman Mason and Sarah Hooper Mason. As noted, Sarah was baptised on 24th March, 1774 (Harvey, 1993). The Prince Regent was born in 1762 and would have been about twelve years old when Sarah was baptised and perhaps seven years old when James was born; this militates against his having been Sarah and James' father. The Prince was about 42 when Sarah's daughter Caroline was born. The Prince's father, George III, would have been some 38 years old when Sarah was conceived but, by that time, he was married with several children.

So the origin of the incorrect bar-sinister myth is unexplained; at the same time, Rev. Mason's and Lady Drake's possessions and life styles do seem to have reflected considerable resources – of course, Thomas Edward Drake was of a prominent Exeter family, but Caroline married him only in 1855. In other words, if the Masons were not the Prince's progeny, the source of the apparent wealth when Masons became Widecombe-in-the-Moor residents remains an interesting mystery.

REFERENCES

Document numbers of items preserved in the following Record Offices are referenced in the text:

DRO - Document in Devon Record Office, Exeter.
PRO - Document in Public Record Office, London.
SAR - Document in Somerset Record Office, Taunton.

Data from the following references have been used:

1851 British Census as cited by Family Historic Resource File, The Church of Jesus Christ of Latter-day Saints, PRO Ref: HO/107/1871, Folio 154, p. 9, FHL Film 0221019, 1997 – searched under address: Bunhill, Widecombe In Moor.

1881 British Census as cited by Intellectual Reserve, Inc., PRO Ref RG11, Piece 2162, Folio 61, p. 7-8, and Folio 63, p. 11, FHL film 1341521, 1999 – search under Dwelling: Bunhill, Bunhill Farm, and Tunhill Farm, Widdecombe in the Moor.

Amery, J. S., 1925, Address of the President: *Trans. Devon. Assoc.*, v. 56 for 1924, pp. 43-102.

Andriette, E. A., 1971, *Devon and Exeter in the Civil War*: David and Charles, Newton Abbot, 237 pp.

Bagehot., 2009, The unfinished revolution: *The Economist*, v. 389, no. 8609, p. 40.

Barber, R., 1992, *Bestiary*: The Folio Society, London, 205 pp.

Baring-Gould, [W.] S., 1899, *A book of the West: being an introduction to Devon and Cornwall: Vol. I. Devon*: Methuen & Co., London, 372 pp.

Baring-Gould, [W.] S., 1900, *A book of Dartmoor* (3rd edit.): Methuen & Co., London, 1916, 283 pp.

Baring-Gould, [W.] S., 1901, *Royal Georgie*: Methuen & Co., London, 333 pp.

Baring-Gould, [W.] S., 1912, *Sheepstor*: Hoyten & Cole, Plymouth, 31 pp.

Baring-Gould, [W.] S., 1890, *Old Country Life*: Methuen & Co., London, 389 pp.

Batten, K., and Bennett, F. B., 1996, *The printed maps of Devon: County maps 1575-1837*: Devon Books, Tiverton, 248 pp.

Beeson, M. M. R., and Masterman, M. C. H., ca. 1979, *An archaeological survey of enclosed land in Widecombe-in-the-Moor Parish*: Devon Committee for Rescue Archaeology, DAS/DCRR Publications, No. 7 (Typescript of 82 pp. but only alternate pages numbered, plus maps).

Augmented by hand-written notes (unknown hand) in the copy in Widecombe-in-the-Moor Parish Chest.

Blome, R., 1681, *Speed's Maps Epitomiz'd*: R. Blome, London.

Booker, F., 1970, Industry: in *Dartmoor: A new study* (edit: C. Gill): David and Charles, Newton Abbot, pp. 100-38.

Brewer, D., 2002, *Dartmoor Boundary Markers and other markers on and around the Moor*: Halsgrove, Tiverton, 320 pp.

Brown, M., 1997, *The Dartmoor Tithe Apportionments, Vol. 5 Buckfastleigh Holne Widecombe Ilsington Manaton*: Dartmoor Press, Plymouth, 14 pp.

Brown, M., 1998a, *Family history & genealogical notes on the Smerdon families of Buckland in the Moor and the neighbouring Parishes of Widecombe, Ilsington & Ashburton c1538 to c1837*: *Part A Introductory Notes - Family trees supplementary indexes*, 32 p.; *Part B Forenames Adelaide to George*, 32 p.; *Part C Forenames Grace to Margaret*, 24 p.; *Part D Forenames Margery to Richard*, 32 p.; *Part E Forenames Robage to Winifred*, 28 p.: Dartmoor Press, Plymouth.

Brown, M., 1998b, A day in the life of the Smerdons of Bonehill and Widecombe: *Dartmoor Newsletter*, no. 43, pp. 25-6.

Butler, J., 1991, *Dartmoor atlas of antiquities: Volume One – The East*: Devon Books (Town & Country Books), Kingskerswell, Devon, 174 pp.

Campbell, J., 1987, Some agents and agencies of the late Anglo-Saxon State: in *Domesday Studies* (edit: Holt, J. C.), Boydell Press, Woodbridge, Suffolk, pp. 201-18.

Campbell, M., 1983, *The English Yeoman under Elizabeth and the early Stuarts* (3rd edit.): Merlin Press, London, 453pp.

Chapple, W., 1785, *A review of part of Risdon's Survey of Devon; containing the General Description of that County; with corrections, annotations, and additions*; E. Thorn, Exeter, 144 pp.

Cocks, J. S., 1970, Saxon and early medieval times: in *Dartmoor: A new study* (edit.: C. Gill), David and Charles, Newton Abbot, pp. 76-99.

Cocks, J. V. S., 1986, Dartmoor Devonshire: in *Local maps and plans from Medieval England* (edit.: Skelton, R. A. and Harvey, P. D. A.): Oxford Univ. Press, Oxford, pp. 293-302.

Coleman, E. C. (edit.), 2006, *The travels of Sir John Mandeville*: Nonsuch Publishing, Stroud, 286 pp.

Cresswell, B. F., 1932, *A book of Devonshire parsons*: Heath Cranton, London, 192 pp.

Crossing, W., 1888, *Amid Devonia's Alps*: Simpkin, Marshall, London, 231 pp.

Crossing, W., 1901, *A hundred years on Dartmoor: historical notices of the Forest and its purlieus during the nineteenth century*: Western Morning News, Plymouth, 132 pp.

Darby, H. C., and Versey, G. R., 1975, *Domesday Gazetteer*: Cambridge Univ. Press, Cambridge, 544 pp.

Davidson, J. B., 1876, Some Anglo-Saxon boundaries now deposited in the Albert Memorial Museum, Exeter: *Trans. Devon. Assoc.*, v. 8, pp. 396-419.

Davis, R. H. C., 1987, Domesday Book: Continental parallels: in *Domesday Studies* (edit.: Holt, J. C.): Boydell Press, Woodbridge, Suffolk, pp. 15-39.

Devon County Council Historic Environment Service, *Historic Landscape Characterisation maps: http://www.devon.gov.uk/index/ environment/historic_environment/landscapes/landscape-characterisation/ historiclandscapecharacterisationmaps.htm*

Devonshire Association, 1884-1892, *The Devonshire Domesday and geld inquest: extensions, translations, and indices*: W. Brendon and Son, Plymouth, vols. 1 & 2, 1236 pp.

Dietz, H., 2005, The eschatological dimension of church architecture: *www.sacredarchitecture.org*

Djabri, S. C., 1991, The making of a legend: *Dartmoor Magazine (Quayside Pubs., Brixham)*, no. 23, pp. 4-6.

Donn, B., 1765, *A Map of the County of Devon with the City and County of Exeter ....*: Benjamin Donn, London (Facsimile: 1965, Devon and Cornwall Record Society & The University of Exeter).

Dymond, R. (edit.), 1875, *The Widecombe Chronicle and Dartmoor Gazette* (2nd edit.): Torquay Directory, Torquay, 8pp.

Dymond, R., 1876, *"Things new and old" concerning the Parish of Widecombe-in-the-Moor and its neighbourhood*: Torquay Directory Co., Torquay, 119 pp.

Finberg, H. P. R., 1969, *West-country historical studies*: David and Charles, Newton Abbot, 232 pp.

Fox, H., 2000, Medieval farming and rural settlement: in *Historical atlas of south-west England*: (edit.: Kain, R., and Ravenhill, W.), Univ. Exeter Press, Exeter, pp. 273-80.

Friends of the Devon Archives, 2007, Freeholders: *www.foda.org.uk/ freeholders*

Gawne, E., 1970, Field patterns in Widecombe Parish and the Forest of Dartmoor: *Trans. Devon. Assoc.*, v. 102, pp. 49-69.

Gawne, E., and Sanders, J., 1998, *Early Dartmoor Farmhouses: Longhouses in Widecombe and some surrounding parishes*: Orchard Publications, Newton Abbot, 98 pp.

Gover, J. E. B., Mawer, A., and Stenton, F. M., (edits.), 1932, *The place names of Devon (Part Two)*: English Place-name Society, vol. IX, Cambridge Univ. Press, 335-754 pp.

Groves, R., 1970, Roads and tracks: in *Dartmoor: A new study* (edit.: C. Gill), David and Charles, Newton Abbot, pp. 182-203.

Harrod, J. G., 1878, *Royal County Directory of Devonshire* (2nd edit.).

Harvey, P. D. A., 1980, *The history of topographical maps: Symbols, pictures and surveys*: Thames and Hudson, London, 199 pp.

Harvey, P. G. T. B., 1993, *In quest of the Drake connection*: typed Ms., 7 pp.

Havinden, M., and Wilkinson, F., 1970, Farming: in *Dartmoor: A new study* (edit.: C. Gill) David and Charles, Newton Abbot, pp. 139-181.

Hemery, E., 1983, *High Dartmoor: Land and people*: Robert Hale, London, 1073 pp.

Hill, Lord G., 1868, *Gweedore*: Phillips & Probert, Worcester, 32 p.

Hinton, I., 2004, Do chancels weep? Does the often noted difference between the alignments of nave and chancel actually mean anything? *Church Archaeology*, v. 5/6, pp. 42-54.

Holt, J. C., 1987, 1086: in *Domesday Studies* (edit.: Holt, J. C.): Boydell Press, Woodbridge, Suffolk, pp. 41-64.

Hoskins, W. G., 1954, *Devon*: Collins Clear-type Press, London, 600 pp.

Jones, G. R. J., 1987, The portrayal of land settlement in Domesday Book: in *Domesday Studies* (edit.: Holt, J. C.): Boydell Press, Woodbridge, Suffolk, pp. 183-200.

Kelly, 1893., *Kelly's Directory of Devonshire & Cornwall*: Kelly & Co., Ltd., London.

Kelly, 1866, 1873, 1883, 1889, 1893, 1897, 1902, 1910, 1914, 1919, 1923, 1926, 1930, 1933, 1935, & 1939, *Directory of Devonshire.*, London.

Kowaleski, M., 1995, *Local markets and regional trade in medieval Exeter*: Cambridge Univ. Press, Cambridge, 442 pp.

Lea, P., 1694, *The Shires of England and Wales*: Philip Lea, London.

Lineham, C. C., 1962, A forgotten manor in Widecombe-in-the-Moor: *Trans. Devon. Assoc.*, v. 94, pp. 463-92.

Loyn, H. R., 1987, The beyond of Domesday Book: in *Domesday Studies* (edit.: Holt, J. C.), Boydell Press, Woodbridge, Suffolk, pp. 1-13.

Lysons, D., and Lysons, S., 1822, *Magna Britannia - being a concise topographical account of the several counties of Great Britain. Volume the sixth containing Devonshire : Topographical and historical account of Devonshire*, Vol. II, Thomas Cadell, London, p. 556.

Maitland, F. W., 1897, *Domesday Book and beyond: three essays in the early history of England*: Cambridge Univ. Press (1960 re-issue, Collins Fontana Library, London, 605 pp., from which page references are cited).

Margary, H., 1977, *The Old Series Ordnance Survey maps of England and Wales Scale 1 inch to 1 mile: A reproduction of the 110 sheets of the survey in early state in 10 volumes: Volume II Devon, Cornwall and West Somerset*: Harry Margary, Lympne Castle, Kent, xliv pp. and 66 plates.

Maxfield, V. A., 2000, The Roman Army: in *Historical Atlas of south-west England* (edit.: Kain, R., and Ravenhill, W.), Univ. Exeter Press, Exeter, pp. 77-9.

Michelmore, Loveys & Sons, 1949, *Auction by Order of the Trustees: The well-known agricultural and sporting Estate - The Bagpark Estate*: Illustrated printed brochure with maps for auction at Commercial Hotel, Newton Abbot, 3 pm., 19 October, 1949.

Millea, N., 2007, *The Gough Map: The earliest road map of Great Britain?* : Bodleian Library, Univ. of Oxford, Oxford, 95 pp.

Miller, E., 1960, Introduction: in *Domesday Book and beyond: three essays in the early history of England* (by Maitland, F. W.): Collins Fontana Library, London, pp. 15-22

Miller, E., and Hatcher, J., 1978, *Medieval England – rural society and economic change 1086-1348*: Longmans Group, London, 302 pp.

Milton, P., 2006, *The discovery of Dartmoor: a wild and wondrous region*: Phillimore & Co., Chichester, 241 pp.

Moore, S. A., 1890, Report: in Moore, S. A. and Birkett, P., *A short history of the Rights of Common upon the Forest of Dartmoor and the Commons of Devon*: Dartmoor Preservation Assoc., Plymouth, 181 pp.

Morden, R., 1676, *The 52 Counties of England and Wales*: Morden, Berry, Green, & Minikin, London.

Moreland, C., and Bannister, D., 1993, *Antique Maps* (Paper Back edit.): Phaidon Press, London, 326 pp.

Morris, C., (edit.), 1982, *The illustrated journeys of Celia Fiennes c. 1682 - c. 1712*: Webb and Bower, Exeter, 248 pp.

Morris and Co., 1870. *Commercial Directory and Gazetteer of Devonshire*

Muirden, J., 2005, Why don't Devon churches face east?: *Trans. Devon. Assoc.*, v. 137, pp. 171-92.

National Gazetteer of Great Britain and Ireland, 1868.

Ogilby, J., 1675, *Britannia, Volume the First: or, an Illustration of the Kingdom of England and Dominion of Wales*: John Ogilby, London, 100 Plates.

Ordnance Survey, 1809, *Devon (Tavistock)* Sheet XXV, State 6, Old Series Maps of England and Wales, 1 inch to 1 mile, The Tower, London.

Ordnance Survey, 1889, *England – Devon*, Sheet 100/SW, 6 inch to 1 mile, Southampton.

Ordnance Survey, 1900, *Dartmoor*, Sheets 324, 338, (1898 Revision), New Series Maps of England and Wales, 1 inch to 1 mile, Southampton.

Ordnance Survey, 1904, *Devonshire* Sheet C (S.W.), (revised 2nd edit), 6 inch to 1 mile map (surveyed in 1884), Southampton.

Ordnance Survey, 1905, England – Devon, Sheet C.14, 2nd edition (SX7177), 25 inch/mile (1:2,500), Southampton.

Ordnance Survey, 1919, *Contoured road map of Dartmoor and Exeter*: Sheet 138, Popular Edition One-Inch Map, Southampton.

Ordnance Survey, 2005, *Dartmoor*: Sheet 28, Outdoor Leisure Series 1:25,000 Map, Southampton.

Ordnance Survey (Ireland), 1906, 6 inch/mile sheet 32 (SE) (2nd edit.), Dublin.

Overton, J., 1685, *Atlas III*: John Overton, London.

Palmer, J. J. N., 1987, The Domesday Manor: in *Domesday Studies* (edit.: Holt, J. C.): Boydell Press, Woodbridge, Suffolk, pp. 139-53.

Pattison, P., 1999, Challacombe revisited: in *Patterns of the past: essays in landscape history for Christopher Taylor* (edit.: Pattison, P., Field, D., and Ainsworth, S.): Oxbow, Oxford, pp. 61-70.

Paris, M., *ca.* 1250, Map of Great Britain: in *History of the English*.

Phillpotts, E., 1913, *Widecombe Fair* (1983 reprint): Anthony Mott, London, 350 pp.

Pike, C., 1993, *Heathercombe: the history of a Dartmoor Valley*: Westcountry Books, Tiverton, 92 pp.

Ravenhill, M. R., and Rowe, M. M., 2000, *Early Devon maps: Maps of lands and estates in Devon before 1700*: Friends of Devon's Archives Occasional Publication Number 1, Exeter, 58 pp.

Ravenhill, M. R., and Rowe, M. M., 2002, *Devon maps and mapmakers: Manuscript maps before 1840* (2 vols.): Devon and Cornwall Record Society, Exeter, v. 43 N.S. (for 2000), 433 pp.

Ravenhill, W., 1992, *Christopher Saxton's 16th century maps*: Chatsworth Library (Airlife Publishing), Shrewsbury, 99 pp.

Reichel, O. J., 1908, The Hundred of Haytor in the time of Testa de Nevil, A.D. 1244: *Trans. Devon. Assoc.*, v. 40, pp. 110-37.

Rennells, P., 1999, North Hall (presentation 1999 and updates): *http//:www.widecombe-in-the moor.com/history/projects/north_hall/north_hall_project.php*

Rennells, P., 2008a, North Hall: *www.widecombe-in-the-moor.com/history/minutes/2008/minutes_may_2008.php*

Rennells, P., 2008b, North Hall 1998-2008: *www.widecombe-in-the-moor.com/history/minutes/2008/north_hall2008.php*

Risdon, T., 1811, *The chorographical description or Survey of the County of Devon* (reprint of 1714 text): Rees and Curtis, London, 442 pp.

Rowe, S., 1896, *A perambulation of the ancient and Royal Forest of Dartmoor and its venville precincts or a topographical survey of their antiquities and scenery* (3rd edit.): James G. Commin, Exeter, 516 pp.

Sandles, T., 2007, The church on the hill: *www.legendarydartmoor.co.uk/buckfastleigh_church.htm*

Saxton, C., 1579, *An Atlas of England and Wales*: London.

Sheldon, G., 1928, *From trackway to turnpike*: Oxford Univ. Press, Oxford, 178 pp.

Smith, L. B., 2006, *Treason in Tudor England: politics and paranoia;* (paperback edit.): Pimlico (Random House), London, 342 pp.

Stanbrook, E., 1996, The building of Princetown Church, Dartmoor: a unique monument to French and American Prisoners of War: *Trans. Devon. Assoc.*, v. 128, pp. 91-100.

Stenton, Sir F. M., 1971, *Anglo-Saxon England* (3rd edit.): Oxford Univ. Press, Oxford, 765 pp.

Thomas, R., 1992, The mysterious Lady Darke: Western Morning News.

Thorn, T., and Thorn, J., 1985, *Domesday Book*, vol. 9 (Devon), Parts 1 and 2: Phillimore & Co., Ltd., Chichester, no page numbers.

Todd, M., 2000, Classical sources for Roman place-names: in *Historical Atlas of south-west England* (edit.: Kain, R. and Ravenhill, W.), Univ. Exeter Press, Exeter, pp. 80-1.

Trewman's Exeter Flying Post, 1867, *To be sold ....;* 25 Sept.1867, Exeter.

Turner, S. C., 2005, *Devon Historic Landscape Characterisation*, 68 pp.: *www.devon.gov.uk/index/environment/historic_environment/landscapes/landscape-characterisation/historiclandscapecharacterisationmethodology.htm*

Turner, S. [C.], 2006, *Making a Christian Landscape: The countryside in early medieval Cornwall, Devon and Wessex*: Exeter Univ. Press, Exeter, 218 pp.

Vancouver, C., 1808, *General view of the agriculture of the County of Devon; with observations on the means of its improvement*: R. Phillips, London, 479 pp. [1969, facsimile edit.: David and Charles, Newton Abbot,]

Waldseemüller, M., 1513, Tabula Nova Hibernie Anglie Et Scotie: double-page map in *Claudii Ptolemei .., Geographiae opus novissima ... MDXIII*, printed by J. Schott, Strassburg.

White, W., 1850, *History, Gazetteer and Directory of Devonshire, and the City and County of Exeter; comprising a general survey of the County of Devon, and the Diocese of Exeter...*: Robert Leader, Sheffield, 804 pp.

White, W., 1878-9, *History, Gazetteer and Directory of the County of Devon including the City of Exeter, and comprising a general survey of the County...*: William White, London, xvi + 1103 pp.

Whitten, E. H. T., 1998, The hamlet of Bonehill: *Dartmoor Newsletter*, no. 42, pp. 36-7

Widecombe Fair [Committee Co. Ltd.], 2003, *Souvenir of Widecombe Fair*, Widecombe-in-the-Moor, 40 pp.

Widecombe and District Local History Group, 2007, *The history of Widecombe Fair*: Orchard Press, Chudleigh, 102 pp.

Widecombe History Group, 2000, Dousing North Hall: *http//:www.widecombe-in-the-moor.com/history/projects/north_hall/dowsing_north_hall.php*

Widecombe History Group, 2004, *Parish Document Search Facility*: CD of updated 2001 database, Widecombe History Group, Widecombe-in-the-Moor.

Widecombe History Group, 2005, Tithe Map project: *http//:www.widecombe-in-the-moor.com/images/map_damage_3.gif*

[Widecombe] Poor Rate Register, July 1890 (Manuscript volume owned by Widecombe-in-the-Moor History Group).

Woods, I., 1977, Memoranda from the Parish Officers' accounts Widecombe-in-the-Moor 1711-1840: *The Devon Historian*, no. 14, pp. 17-20.

Woods, I. M., 1971, Widecombe-in-the-Moor – a parochial jigsaw: *Trans. Devon. Assoc.*, v. 103, pp. 254-7.

Woods, S. H., 1988, *Dartmoor Stone*: Devon Books, Exeter, 311 pp.

Woods, S. H., 1996, *Widecombe-in-the-Moor: A pictorial history of the Dartmoor village*: Devon Books, Tiverton, 160 pp.

Woods, S. [H.], 2000, *Uncle Tom Cobley and all: Widecombe-in-the-Moor*: Halsgrove, Tiverton, 144 pp.

Worth, R. H., 1967, *Worth's Dartmoor (new edit.)*: (edit.: Spooner, G. M.), David and Charles, Newton Abbot, 523 pp.

Worth, R. N., 1892?, *Suggested identifications of the Domesday Manors of Devon*: A 'first proof' printed for Devon. Assoc. Domesday Committee before 1893, 29 pp.

Worthy, C., 1874, *Widecombe-in-the-Moor*: The Daily Western Times for 11.4.1874.

Worthy, C., 1875, *Ashburton and its neighbourhood or the antiquities and history of the Borough of Ashburton*: L. B. Varder, Ashburton, 160+36 pp. [Chap. IX: Widecombe-in-the-Moor]

Wright, Sir M., 1730, *An introduction to the Law of Tenures*, London.